by Country at the end of The 2009 Race to Dubai

The European Tour International Schedule embraces the world. In total no fewer than 37 countries have hosted competition on The European Tour and players from no fewer than 35 countries have become Tour champions. The year of 1971 officially marked the birth of The European Tour and following the inaugural Race to Dubai in November, 2009, there had been in total 374 champions.

29 SWITZERLAND
Number of wins: 1
Number of winners: 1
Leading performer: André Bossert (1)

30 TAIWAN
Number of wins: 2
Number of winners: 2
Leading performer: Yeh Wei-tze,
Lin Wen-tang (1)

31 THAILAND
Number of wins: 6
Number of winners: 3
Leading performers:
Thongchai Jaidee (4); Chapchai Nirat,
Thaworn Wiratchant (1)

32 TRINIDAD and TOBAGO
Number of wins: 2
Number of winners: 1
Leading performer: Stephen Ames (2).

19 KOREA
Number of wins: 4
Number of winners: 3
Leading performers:
Y E Yang (2); KJ Choi, Charlie Wi (1)

20 THE NETHERLANDS
Number of wins: 4
Number of winners: 3
Leading performers: Robert-Jan
Derksen (2); Maarten Lafeber,
Rolf Muntz (1).

21 NEW ZEALAND
Number of wins: 25
Number of winners: 7
Leading performers: Michael Campbell
(8); Frank Nobilo (5); Bob Charles,
Greg Turner (4)

22 NORTHERN IRELAND
Number of wins: 34
Number of winners: 7
Leading performers: Darren Clarke (12);
Ronan Rafferty (7); David Feherty (5)

23 PORTUGAL
Number of wins: 1
Number of winners: 1
Leading performer: Daniel Silva (1)

24 SCOTLAND
Number of wins: 125
Number of winners: 20
Leading performers: Colin
Montgomerie (31); Sam Torrance (21);
Sandy Lyle (18)

25 SINGAPORE
Number of wins: 1
Number of winners: 1
Leading performer: Mardan Mamat (1)

26 SOUTH AFRICA
Number of wins: 89
Number of winners: 26
Leading performers: Ernie Els (24);
Retief Goosen (14); Hugh Baiocchi (6)

27 SPAIN
Number of wins: 150
Number of winners: 28
Leading performers: Seve Ballesteros
(50); José Maria Olazábal (23);
Miguel Angel Jiménez (15)

28 SWEDEN
Number of wins: 83
Number of winners: 27
Leading performers: Robert Karlsson
(9); Niclas Fasth, Anders Forsbrand,
Per-Ulrik Johansson, Henrik Stenson (6)

33 USA
Number of wins: 116
Number of winners: 51
Leading performers: Tiger Woods (38);
Phil Mickelson (6); Tom Watson (5);
Bob Byman, Mark O'Meara (4)

34 WALES
Number of wins: 43
Number of winners: 8
Leading performers: Ian Woosnam
(29); Stephen Dodd, Phillip Price (3)

35 ZIMBABWE
Number of wins: 29
Number of winners: 3
Leading performers: Mark McNulty
(16); Nick Price (7); Tony Johnstone (6)

MOST VICTORIES BY COUNTRY
THE TOP TEN

1.	England	249
2.	Spain	150
3.	Scotland	125
4.	USA	118
5.	Australia	102
6.	South Africa	89
7.	Sweden	83
8.	Germany	56
9.	Ireland	46
10.	Wales	43

The European Tour
Yearbook 2010

OFFICIAL PUBLICATION

Introduction from The European Tour

Lee Westwood's superb triumph in the inaugural Race to Dubai was one of many history making achievements on The 2009 European Tour International Schedule highlighted in this, the 22nd edition of The European Tour Yearbook.

The success of The 2009 Race to Dubai, culminating in Lee finishing ahead of Rory McIlroy, Martin Kaymer, Ross Fisher and Paul Casey, can be traced to the astute professionalism and dedication of many people including our partners at Leisurecorp, a division of Nakheel Leisure.

We would first and foremost congratulate all the Members of The European Tour who, by embracing the new season-long competition with their unique skills, brought true resonance to the Royal and Ancient game.

Golfers from more than 40 countries visited no fewer than 27 destinations and played in 51 tournaments on The 2009 European Tour International Schedule, elevating and enhancing the sport's reputation worldwide.

The denouement of our season came at the Dubai World Championship some 382 days after The Race to Dubai had started and Lee's return to Number One – a position he previously held in 2000 – enabled him to regain The Harry Vardon Trophy, awarded annually to the leading player in The Race to Dubai.

Lee earned €4,237,762 – the highest single season earnings in European Tour history – during a year in which he was one shot away from a play-off in The Open Championship, tied third in the US PGA Championship and won the Portugal Masters in addition to the Dubai World Championship presented by: DP World.

Our Members regard the winning of each and every tournament as a title to cherish and in 2009 no fewer than six – Paul Casey, sadly denied the chance of playing the Dubai World Championship because of injury, Simon Dyson, Thongchai Jaidee, Martin Kaymer, Richard Sterne and Westwood himself – enjoyed the delight of winning on two occasions.

In 2009 there were also, from ten different countries, no fewer than 15 first time winners – Rafael Cabrera-Bello, Tano Goya, Lucas Glover, Oskar Henningsson, Michael Hoey, Jeppe Huldahl, Anthony Kang, Danny Lee, Shane Lowry, Ross McGowan, Rory McIlroy, Christian Nilsson, Alex Noren, Rod Pampling and Lin Wen-tang. Danny and Shane also made history by becoming only the second and third amateurs to win on The European Tour International Schedule. We also congratulate Chris Wood on becoming The Sir Henry Cotton Rookie of the Year.

History was also made when Angel Cabrera became the first player from South America to win the Masters Tournament and Y E Yang became the first Asian golfer to win a Major Championship at the US PGA Championship. Furthermore, at the age of 59, Tom Watson was a finger touch away from a truly romantic victory at Turnberry where he lost in a play-off to Stewart Cink for The 138th Open Championship.

Sam Torrance, at the age of 56, did write his name in the record books by narrowly finishing in front of Ian Woosnam on the European Senior Tour Order of Merit to claim his third John Jacobs Trophy. On the European Challenge Tour, Edoardo Molinari was the undisputed number one. He won three times, earned a record €242,979 and advanced 569 places on the Official World Golf Ranking. As a result, Edoardo and his younger brother Francesco will both start The 2010 European Tour International Schedule among the top 100 players in the world.

For Sir Terry Matthews, the visionary Welsh businessman, the playing of The 2010 Ryder Cup at The Celtic Manor Resort will fulfil an ambition and make history with the contest taking place for the first time at a venue – The Twenty Ten Course – designed specifically for the biennial match between Europe and the United States. We wish the Captains – Colin Montgomerie and Corey Pavin – and the 24 players all the very best.

Golf is played in virtually every country in the world and we welcomed, in October 2009, another history making decision when the International Olympic Committee admitted golf into the Olympic Games. Many international bodies, federations, individuals and indeed players encouraged The European Tour to take a leadership position in securing the Olympic dream and Padraig Harrington, in participating in the final presentation in Copenhagen, stressed his opinion that the competition would evolve and become a huge target for all players once every four years.

We believe that being part of the Olympic Games will create an enthralling new challenge for the players and we will continue, through The European Tour International Schedule, to lead in the development and growth of the game in every corner of the globe.

George O'Grady
Chief Executive
The European Tour

ACKNOWLEDGEMENTS

Executive Editor
Mitchell Platts

Deputy Executive Editor
Scott Crockett

Production Editor
Frances Jennings

Editorial Consultant
Chris Plumridge

Picture Editors
Andrew Redington
Rob Harborne

Art Direction
Tim Leney
Andrew Wright
TC Communications Ltd

Print Managed by
Peter Dane
Mark Baldwin
The Print House Ltd

The European Tour Yearbook 2010 is published by The PGA European Tour, Wentworth Drive, Virginia Water, Surrey GU25 4LX. Distributed through Aurum Press Ltd. 7 Greenland Street London NW1 0ND

© PGA European Tour.

CONTENTS

First Past the Post

It ended, as we had hoped, with a roar of approval after one of the finest rounds in modern golfing history.

Sergio Garcia

DUBAI 1,553,580 yards

SHANGHAI HSBC Champions

The simple fact is that for Lee John Westwood, the inaugural Race to Dubai climaxed with the sweetest of saunters up the final fairway of the Earth course at Jumeirah Golf Estates in the heart of the United Arab Emirates. A saunter, yes, but for the Englishman and everyone else on The European Tour, this Race had been the most competitive and compelling of marathons.

Conceived in 2007, activated in 2008 and brilliantly executed in 2009, The Race To Dubai was, in the end, much more than the sum of its considerable parts. The money is a huge part of it, of course, and the fact that Westwood ended the year with €4,237,762 – the highest single season earnings in European Tour history – should not be overlooked.

But money cannot buy everything. What it does is focus the mind, offer a target and, in this case, encourage the sort of sporting entertainment and endeavour that was set so excellently before a world stage.

While the enthralling Dubai World Championship was the final chapter, the narrative of this story had been written across twelve months, 51 tournaments and 27 destinations in almost every corner of the globe.

When The European Tour took its first tentative steps outside the continent from which it takes its name, there were those who forecast tears. They were right too - but these tears were, ultimately, of joy and were

Lee and Billy Foster

ONE LESS MOVING PART
TO YOUR SWING.

SYNR·G.

More control. More power. More confidence.
Introducing the most stable FootJoy® shoes ever. Get locked in and let it rip.

HARRINGTON AND FOOTJOY. A PERFECT SYNR-G!
Padraig Harrington is wearing SYNR-G shoes in 2009.

Explore footjoy.co.uk/synrg Sign up to The Comfort Zone, our free e-newsletter, at thecomfortzone.info

#1 SHOE IN GOLF

glistening in the eyes of Westwood as the stoical Englishman holed his final putt to win both the week and the year after the most captivating performance of his career.

No-one now may legitimately doubt the wisdom of The European Tour hierarchy about undertaking such a venture. When Chief Executive George O'Grady spoke at the launch in Dubai in November 2007, his happiness was plain to see. Such pleasure was richly deserved while the foresight of the Tour's partners in the venture, Leisurecorp, was commended.

Theirs, naturally, was a business decision but it was a strategy that revolved precisely around the integrity and quality offered by the body of men, players and employees, of The European Tour. In an age when even the most respected of competitors can stoop to underhand methods to secure victory in other sports, the old game's spiritual core of decency once more shines significantly as a beacon of hope in an otherwise beleaguered sporting landscape.

So it was that Rory McIlroy, the new, tousle-haired, and smiley face of much that is in the future for European golf, could play his heart out in Dubai, lose to Westwood and immediately offer sincere words of congratulations to the man who beat him to the biggest of prizes.

He is not alone either. There exists a platoon of young European Tour players who are on the verge of becoming the new, elite force of professional golf over the next decade. Players like Germany's Martin Kaymer and Ross Fisher of England who arrived in Dubai with their own chances of winning the Race before settling for third and fourth place respectively. There are also the likes of Spain's Gonzalo Fernandez-Castaño and Alvaro Quiros, England's Ross McGowan and Oliver Wilson, Italy's

Francesco Molinari and Sweden's Alexander Noren, all in their 20s, to consider in addition to another Englishman, Chris Wood, who celebrated his 22nd birthday by being named The Sir Henry Cotton Rookie of the Year. It is truly a richly embroidered future, especially as, at the end of the inaugural Race to Dubai, six Europeans – Lee Westwood, Paul Casey, Padraig Harrington, Henrik Stenson, Sergio Garcia and Rory McIlroy – occupied places in the top ten of the Official World Golf Ranking for the first time in history.

Why should this be? There are many reasons, not least the legacy offered by older players of the calibre of José Maria Olazábal, who was elected to the World Golf Hall of Fame in 2009, but also there has been the raising of the bar throughout The European Tour when it comes to conditioning and preparation of courses, the improved organisation and prize money, to offer a bedrock of explanation. In all of this, however, the concept of The Race To Dubai is crucial.

Lee and Laurae Westwood

Rory McIlroy

Think It Possible.™

As a Genworth Financial brand ambassador Ross Fisher
exemplifies everything in our Think It Possible culture. He is
clearly focused on achievement, performing at the highest level
and with a desire to be a leader in his field. This is what it means
to Think It Possible. To learn more, visit genworth.com.

Genworth® Financial

Ross Fisher *2008 European Open Champion*

The official sponsor of The European Tour Statistics.

Every journey needs a destination and in Dubai and the Earth course, the Tour found a perfect end-game.

It was a journey that had begun more than a year earlier when Sergio Garcia triumphed in the HSBC Champions in Shanghai. Garcia's mercurial flamboyance meant he led the standings in The Race to Dubai for 11 heady weeks. In all, six players enjoyed the spotlight that comes from being in pole position.

Geoff Ogilvy also led for 11 weeks following his victory in the World Golf Championships - Accenture Match Play; Paul Casey was there for 12 weeks thanks to his wins in The Abu Dhabi Golf Championship and the flagship BMW PGA Championship at Wentworth Club in England; Martin Kaymer was top for six weeks following his back-to-back summer successes in the Open de France ALSTOM and The Barclays Scottish Open, before McIlroy and Westwood grappled with each other so thrillingly over the final couple of months.

Here, sympathetic words must be offered to both Casey and Kaymer for the Englishman and the German each suffered injuries at crucial times. Casey's pulled muscle under his rib cage eventually forced him to withdraw from Dubai while the foot Kaymer hurt while go-karting took him out of competition for nine weeks and numbed his challenge.

They will unquestionably be back to joust again for one of the richest prizes in world sport but only one man could win the first Race to Dubai and so anoint himself the Number One golfer in Europe:- that man was Westwood. It was an achievement which brought the ultimate satisfaction to a professional golfer who has always been a credit to himself, his family and his sport.

Framed by the desert and lost wonderfully in his own cocoon of

A proud José Maria Olazábal displays his World Golf Hall of Fame exhibits with mother, Julia, and father, Gaspar

concentration during the week of the Dubai World Championship, Westwood's golf was simply magnificent. On an Earth course designed by Greg Norman, the lad from Worksop at times touched a game even he did not suspect he possessed.

It was in 2000 that he won his other European Number One title. He was 27 at the time and accepted the triumph as just another happy milestone in a career that already was studded with high success. He had, after all, been runner-up to Colin Montgomerie a year earlier.

However, just when it seemed things could only get better, everything started to turn worse. By 2002 he was in a slump, hovering outside the top 200 in the world and generally fed up with the game. It was, make no mistake, a desperate time for a decent young man. He suddenly portrayed a confused figure in a world he had once strode across with confidence.

An intelligent man, he knew he had a choice to make. He could either walk away from the sport that had already made him comfortable financially or he could face up to the unexpected

Chris Wood

Martin Kaymer

frailties and rededicate himself to improvement. He chose the latter.

He rebuilt his swing under the guidance of his long-time coach Pete Cowen before embarking on a physical fitness campaign that further bolstered both his swing and his ability to maintain energy and focus over the demanding final holes of any fiercely contested tournament week.

This, of course, was the easy bit. The tough part was restoring confidence in his ability. This was something he never had had to worry about as he swashbuckled his way from outstanding youth to precocious professional. It is, however, what separates the talented from the truly successful. It took some time coming, this confidence thing, but when it did, it was an even better and more consistent player who emerged.

Before 2009, he had won 18 European Tour titles but only four of those came after 2000 and no-one knew this weary statistic better than the man himself. However, his instinct to acknowledge the hard facts is a huge strength. Too many sportsmen fool themselves that they are better than they actually are but Westwood, while internally acknowledging his ability,

was determined to remain reluctant to reach out for a trumpet until there was actually something to toot about.

The first stepping stone to that came on Sunday October 18 when he won the Portugal Masters in Vilamoura, his first victory for over two years. The win did more than simply lift him up the rankings, it offered the conclusive evidence he needed that he was not just an outstanding player but, actually, a natural winner. This effect was seen in his stellar performance in Dubai, an effort that was encouraged all the way by his brilliant caddie, Billy Foster.

You see, for Lee Westwood, the big effort in 2009 was not just to make The European Tour's climactic week as a genuine contender but to prove something to himself. It turned out he proved much more.

Asked by a journalist at his post-tournament press conference how good his play had been over a stunning weekend, he at last grabbed that trumpet and tooted: "That was my best ever."

It was good to hear.

Bill Elliott
The Observer

Paul Casey

Geoff Ogilvy

Lee and Andrew Chandler

THE 2009 RACE TO DUBAI FINAL STANDINGS

			€
1	**LEE WESTWOOD**		**4,237,762**
2	Rory McIlroy		3,610,020
3	Martin Kaymer		2,864,342
4	Ross Fisher		2,531,183
5	Paul Casey		2,362,947
6	Geoff Ogilvy		2,202,814
7	Oliver Wilson		2,010,158
8	Simon Dyson		1,807,753
9	Ian Poulter		1,773,470
10	Sergio Garcia		1,660,788
11	Ernie Els		1,571,577
12	Ross McGowan		1,558,808
13	Søren Kjeldsen		1,529,253
14	Francesco Molinari		1,505,010
15	Padraig Harrington		1,468,232

HSBC ◆X

HSBC CHAMPIONS
Sheshan International Golf Club
Shanghai, China
November 6-9, 2008

1	**SERGIO GARCIA**		**66**	**68**	**72**	**68**	**274**	**-14**
2	Oliver Wilson		67	68	69	70	274	-14
3	Peter Hanson		69	70	70	66	275	-13
	Geoff Ogilvy		70	65	70	70	275	-13
5	Henrik Stenson		65	69	72	71	277	-11
6	Charl Schwartzel		69	72	67	70	278	-10
	Adam Scott		66	71	71	70	278	-10
8	Prayad Marksaeng		68	70	71	70	279	-9
	Phil Mickelson		66	70	70	73	279	-9
10	Alvaro Quiros		70	67	73	70	280	-8

Richard Yorke, CEO, HSBC China and Sergio Garcia

Total Prize Fund €3,893,751   **First Prize** €650,382

"I am so proud to win this wonderful tournament. It has been a great week and a superb start to The Race to Dubai"
— Sergio Garcia

Robert Karlsson

Sudden-Death Sergio

It was heralded as the most exciting and significant development in world golf and the start of The Race to Dubai – the HSBC Champions in Shanghai – certainly lived up to that billing. A thrilling finalé saw Spaniard Sergio Garcia lift the title and the gleaming trophy after a sudden-death play-off with his European Ryder Cup colleague Oliver Wilson of England.

Wilson, seeking his maiden European Tour triumph, held sway going into the final round, a shot clear of Australian Geoff Ogilvy and two in front of defending champion Phil Mickelson of America, Sweden's Henrik Stenson and Garcia.

However, the Spaniard successfully made up the ground on the Englishman, a birdie at the closing hole sealing a fine 68 which matched Wilson's 14 under par total of 274.

On the first return to the 18th hole, par fives from both players saw the drama continue but at the second time of asking it was Garcia who produced the shots that mattered; a sublime pitch to ten feet behind the pin and an assured putt for a birdie four giving the 28 year old from Castellon his eighth European Tour International Schedule success. He had moved to the top of The Race to Dubai.

Henrik Stenson

Peter Hanson

Oliver Wilson

Alvaro Quiros

15

 UBS

UBS HONG KONG OPEN
Hong Kong Golf Club
Fanling, Hong Kong
November 20–23, 2008

1	**LIN WEN-TANG**		65	69	64	67	**265**	**-15**
2	Rory McIlroy		70	64	66	65	265	-15
	Francesco Molinari		66	67	67	65	265	-15
4	Pablo Larrazábal		69	67	64	67	267	-13
	Chawalit Plaphol		66	66	70	65	267	-13
6	David Gleeson		72	65	65	66	268	-12
	Bernhard Langer		69	67	63	69	268	-12
	Iain Steel		68	68	66	66	268	-12
	Richard Sterne		64	69	69	66	268	-12
	Oliver Wilson		66	66	65	71	268	-12

Chi-Won Yoon, Country Head and CEO, UBS AG Hong Kong Branch and Lin Wen-tang

Total Prize Fund €1,996,575   **First Prize** €327,383

"This is my first European Tour win and, right now, my feelings cannot be described. All I can do is, hopefully, use my smile to say thank you to everyone"
— Lin Wen-tang

Francesco Molinari

Chinese Cracker

The Race to Dubai promised excitement and thrills on The European Tour International Schedule and, for the second week running, it provided just that in terms of a pulsating extra-holes drama to decide the title. Once the dust had settled on the 50th UBS Hong Kong Open, it was Chinese Taipei's Lin Wen-tang who was smiling, having seen off the challenge of Northern Ireland's Rory McIlroy and Francesco Molinari of Italy to triumph.

A solid first three rounds saw Lin head into the final day in second place, sandwiched between leader Oliver Wilson – hoping to go one better than his play-off defeat to Sergio Garcia in the HSBC Champions – and a resurgent Bernhard Langer – the

winning 2004 Ryder Cup Captain having stormed into contention with a sensational third round 63.

However, with neither the Englishman nor the German able to sustain their respective challenges, it was left to the fast finishing McIlroy and Molinari to tie Lin on 15 under par 265 at the end of regulation play. On the first return to the 18th hole, birdies from Lin and McIlroy were sufficient to end Molinari's involvement, before a second birdie three from the man from Hsinchu City on the same hole moments later – after a stunning approach finished a mere foot from the pin – was good enough for his maiden European Tour title.

Rory McIlroy

Bernhard Langer

George O'Grady, Chief Executive of The European Tour and Joe Guerrisi, UPS Vice President Marketing Asia Pacific Region, celebrate the naming of UPS as the Official Logistics and Express Sponsor of The European Tour

UPS is proud to sponsor the European Tour

SPORTSBET AUSTRALIAN MASTERS

Huntingdale Golf Club
Melbourne, Australia

November 27–30, 2008

1	ROD PAMPLING		71	68	70	67	276	-12
2	Marcus Fraser		73	67	71	65	276	-12
3	Robert Allenby		73	66	67	73	279	-9
4	Tim Clark		67	70	76	67	280	-8
	Nathan Green		72	68	70	70	280	-8
	Alexander Noren		73	71	68	68	280	-8
7	David McKenzie		72	70	71	68	281	-7
8	Martin Erlandsson		74	71	70	67	282	-6
	Marc Leishman		71	70	74	67	282	-6
	Anthony Summers		70	68	71	73	282	-6

Matthew Tripp, CEO of Sportsbet and Rod Pampling

Total Prize Fund €738,851   **First Prize** €140,193

17
425m
PAR 4

"It is great to win on home soil and particularly the Masters which is such a great event. I knew I was hitting the ball well and I hit a lot of great shots this week" — Rod Pampling

Marcus Fraser

Robert Allenby

Steve Webster

Tim Clark

Happy as a Sandboy

For the third week in succession on The 2009 European Tour International Schedule, extra holes were required to determine the champion with home favourite Rod Pampling emerging victorious from the tussle with his fellow countryman Marcus Fraser for the Sportsbet Australian Masters.

Going into the final round on Melbourne's famous sandbelt, the vastly experienced two time champion Robert Allenby was favourite with the sponsors to claim the Gold Jacket for a third occasion, sharing the lead as he did with another Australian, Michael Sim. But, as both men failed to break par, Pampling and Fraser emerged to claim centre stage, ending tied together on 12 under par 276.

Having finished some 45 minutes ahead of Pampling, Fraser spent the time ensuring his heavily pregnant wife Carlie – who had visited hospital earlier in the day as a precaution – did not get over-excited greenside. She held on, as did Pampling, who matched Fraser's tally before winning on the duo's third visit to the demanding 448 yard 18th which had only seen one birdie all day. Not surprising then that Pampling won with a par four as Fraser three putted for a bogey five. A happy ending then for Pampling, but also for the Frasers in early January when little Archie arrived safe and sound.

ALFRED DUNHILL CHAMPIONSHIP
Leopard Creek Country Club
Mpumalanga, South Africa
December 11-14, 2008

1	**RICHARD STERNE**		68	66	68	69	271	-17
2	Johan Edfors		66	69	71	66	272	-16
	Robert Rock		66	67	69	70	272	-16
4	Thomas Aiken		72	65	61	75	273	-15
	Rafael Cabrera-Bello		66	71	68	68	273	-15
6	Keith Horne		70	69	65	70	274	-14
	Alan McLean		68	74	66	66	274	-14
8	Robert Dinwiddie		69	70	68	68	275	-13
	Oskar Henningsson		69	64	69	73	275	-13
	Michael Jonzon		65	72	70	68	275	-13
	David Lynn		68	68	66	73	275	-13
	Tyrone Mordt		68	67	68	72	275	-13
	Alvaro Velasco		68	69	67	71	275	-13

L-R: Gaynor Rupert , wife of Johann Rupert, Chairman of Richemont International , Richard Sterne and Thabang Makwetla, Premier of Mpumalanga

Total Prize Fund €1,000,200   **First Prize** €158,500

"Winning at Leopard Creek in front of my own people will live with me forever. What a magnificent course, place and occasion. The Alfred Dunhill Championship is unforgettable" — Richard Sterne

Thomas Aiken

Robert Rock

Johan Edfors

Final Relief

Every champion feels a huge surge of delight when the winning putt drops on the final green; for Richard Sterne, in the Alfred Dunhill Championship, there was an additional feeling of relief.

For a man who had been ultra consistent elsewhere all week at the Mpumalanga venue, the 541 yard 18th had proved a thorn in his side, dropping five shots in three days thanks to a triple bogey eight on Friday and a double bogey seven on Saturday.

Therefore it said much for the South African's excellence elsewhere – he only dropped three shots in total on all other holes over the four days aside from making 23 birdies and one eagle – that when he

notched a par five on the 18th on Sunday for a closing 69, it was sufficient for a one shot victory over Sweden's Johan Edfors and Robert Rock of England on 17 under par 271.

Sterne had not begun the final round as favourite, that tag being shared by his fellow countryman and third round leader Thomas Aiken and the man just behind him in second place, American Len Mattiace. They might have started with daylight between them and the rest of the field but when they both failed to capitalise on their positions in the final round, it left the door open for the chasing pack with Sterne more than happy to walk through it.

SOUTH AFRICAN OPEN CHAMPIONSHIP
Pearl Valley Golf Estates
Paarl, Western Cape, South Africa
December 18-21, 2008

1	**RICHARD STERNE**		**72**	**69**	**67**	**66**	**274**	**-14**
2	Gareth Maybin		66	69	69	70	274	-14
3	Ernie Els		67	67	77	64	275	-13
	Rory McIlroy		70	68	67	70	275	-13
	Lee Westwood		66	68	68	73	275	-13
6	Richard Finch		69	70	71	66	276	-12
	Retief Goosen		70	66	69	71	276	-12
	Branden Grace		69	67	73	67	276	-12
	Chris Wood		68	69	71	68	276	-12
10	Trevor Immelman		69	71	70	67	277	-11

Gareth Tindall, Commissioner of the Sunshine Tour and Richard Sterne

Total Prize Fund €1,007,670   **First Prize** €158,500

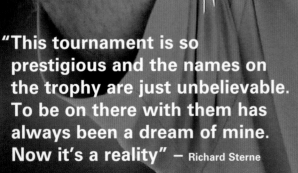

"This tournament is so prestigious and the names on the trophy are just unbelievable. To be on there with them has always been a dream of mine. Now it's a reality" — Richard Sterne

Lee Westwood

Trevor Immelman is presented with Honorary Life Membership of The European Tour by Keith Waters, the Director of International Policy for The European Tour, in recognition of his 2008 Masters Tournament victory

Ernie Els

Gareth Maybin

Double Delight

There is an old adage about buses - you can wait ages for one to come along and then two come along at once. Richard Sterne knows exactly that feeling.

The 27 year old from Pretoria had seen nearly a year pass by from his Joburg Open win to his victory in the Alfred Dunhill Championship, yet had to wait a mere seven days from crowning his success at Leopard Creek to lifting further European Tour silverware in the South African Open Championship.

As he had done seven days earlier Sterne entered the final round off the pace, set by Lee Westwood, but when the Englishman

slipped back on the final day, Sterne's excellent closing 66 saw him move through the field to set the clubhouse mark of 14 under par 274. It was a target very nearly attained by Ernie Els with a stunning closing 64 but the four time winner fell one stroke short, leaving Northern Ireland's Gareth Maybin to force extra holes with Sterne after his final round 70.

The duo returned to the 18th hole but the play-off was brief after Maybin's drive found sand. The man from Belfast splashed out and did well to make a par five, but when Sterne chipped to three feet with his third shot and holed out for a birdie four, the title was his.

"After the start I made, I was thinking 'what's this?' but I was proud of my recovery and I'm delighted to win. I thought 15 under par might be the mark, and I was right" – Anders Hansen

Joburg Open 2009

JOBURG OPEN
Royal Johannesburg and Kensington Golf Club
(East Course and West Course)
Johannesburg, South Africa
January 8–11, 2009

1	**ANDERS HANSEN**		71	68	64	66	269	-15
2	Andrew McLardy		65	68	69	68	270	-14
3	David Drysdale		65	66	71	69	271	-13
4	Charl Schwartzel		68	71	63	70	272	-12
	Tyrone Van Aswegen		69	65	70	68	272	-12
	Danny Willett		67	66	71	68	272	-12
7	David Dixon		68	69	68	68	273	-11
	Joakim Haeggman		69	68	66	70	273	-11
	Richard McEvoy		69	65	72	67	273	-11
10	Tano Goya		70	69	69	66	274	-10
	Louis Oosthuizen		71	66	67	70	274	-10

Anders Hansen and Mavela Dlamini, Johannesburg City Manager

Total Prize Fund €1,121,436   **First Prize** €174,350

David Drysdale

Charl Schwartzel

Fine Finish

It has been said many times that it is not how you start which is important, rather how you finish, and one man who would concur completely with that statement is Anders Hansen in terms of the 2009 Joburg Open.

It is doubtful whether any of the 210 competitors who began the tournament made a worse start than the 38 year old who double bogeyed the opening hole on the East Course and followed that with a bogey four at the second. Three over par after two holes is not championship winning material but the winner of two BMW PGA Championship titles at Wentworth Club is made of stern stuff and battled back to end round one at level par.

After that, however, it was a different story for the Dane who peppered his card with birdies for the remaining three days; posted three rounds in the 60s – the highlight of which was his third round 64 on the same East Course – to finish one shot clear of South Africa's Andrew McLardy.

Highlight of his final round was a run of four birdies in a row from the sixth which moved him into pole position before he cemented victory with a fine birdie four on the 551 yard 18th hole. It truly was a fine finish.

Danny Willett

Andrew McLardy

THE ROYAL TROPHY
Amata Spring Country Club
Bangkok, Thailand
January 9–11, 2009

"We are thrilled to win but it was a great three days which featured some wonderful golf from the players of both sides – I know the spectators loved every minute"

— Naomichi 'Joe' Ozaki

Total Prize Fund €1,074,430

ASIA (Captain: Naomichi 'Joe' Ozaki)		EUROPE: (Captain: José Maria Olazábal)	
Friday Foursomes:			
R Ishikawa (JPN) & T Taniguchi (JPN)	0	P Lawrie (SCO) & S Hansen (DEN) (2 and 1)	1
C Wi (KOR) & L Wen-chong (CHN) (2 holes)	1	P McGinley (IRL) & P Larrazabal (ESP)	0
H Tanihara (JPN) & S K Ho (KOR) (1 hole)	1	N Dougherty (ENG) & O Wilson (ENG)	0
T Jaidee (THA) & P Marksaeng (THA) (5 and 4)	1	N Fasth (SWE) & J Edfors (SWE)	0
Session Score:	3		1
Match Position:	3		1
Saturday Fourballs:			
R Ishikawa & T Taniguchi (halved)	½	P Lawrie & S Hansen (halved)	½
C Wi & L Wen-chong (3 and 2)	1	N Dougherty & O Wilson	0
H Tanihara & S K Ho (2 and 1)	1	N Fasth & J Edfors	0
T Jaidee & P Marksaeng (4 and 2)	1	P McGinley & P Larrazabal	0
Session Score:	3½		½
Match Position:	6½		1½
Sunday Singles:			
R Ishikawa (halved)	½	S Hansen (halved)	½
L Wen-chong	0	P Lawrie (3 and 2)	1
C Wi	0	N Dougherty (1 hole)	1
P Marksaeng (5 and 4)	1	P Larrazabal	0
H Tanihara	0	O Wilson (3 and 2)	1
S K Ho	0	J Edfors (5 and 4)	1
T Taniguchi (7 and 6)	1	N Fasth	0
T Jaidee (5 and 4)	1	P McGinley	0
Session Score:	3½		4½
ASIA	**10**	**EUROPE**	**6**

Per player winning Team €76,105   **Per player losing Team €38,052**

Third Time Lucky

It was a case of third time lucky for Asia as they claimed their first victory over Europe in The Royal Trophy.

After having lost the first two stagings of the contest in 2006 and 2007, Asia – captained for the second time by Japanese golfing great Naomichi 'Joe' Ozaki – were always in control against the José Maria Olazábal-led European side, winning both the Friday foursomes and the Saturday fourballs to set up a five point lead going into Sunday's singles. It left Asia requiring only two points from the eight ties and, although Europe won the session 4 ½ - 3 ½, Asia comfortably claimed overall victory by 10-6.

The 2008 contest had been postponed due to the death of the King of Thailand's sister, while the rescheduling coincided with the start of Seve Ballesteros' recovery from brain surgery – the five time Major Champion being the man behind the whole concept of The Royal Trophy itself. Ballesteros sent a moving message to both teams which was read out at the Opening Ceremony and Olazábal spoke for everyone when he said; "All our thoughts and prayers are with Seve in his recovery battle."

Paul Lawrie

Pablo Larrazabal and José Maria Olazábal

ABU DHABI GOLF CHAMPIONSHIP
Abu Dhabi Golf Club
Abu Dhabi, UAE
January 15–18, 2009

His Highness Sheikh Sultan Bin Tahnoon Al Nahyan, Chairman, Abu Dhabi Tourism Authority and Paul Casey

Total Prize Fund €1,475,158   **First Prize** €245,122

#	Player		R1	R2	R3	R4	Total	Par
1	**PAUL CASEY**		69	65	63	70	267	-21
2	Martin Kaymer		68	68	65	67	268	-20
	Louis Oosthuizen		67	69	68	64	268	-20
4	Anthony Wall		67	67	69	67	270	-18
5	Johan Edfors		66	69	69	67	271	-17
	Padraig Harrington		71	66	68	66	271	-17
	Rory McIlroy		66	69	71	65	271	-17
8	Sergio Garcia		70	71	67	64	272	-16
	Danny Willett		71	66	68	67	272	-16
10	Bradley Dredge		71	69	66	67	273	-15
	Peter Hanson		67	71	66	69	273	-15
	Francesco Molinari		67	69	71	66	273	-15

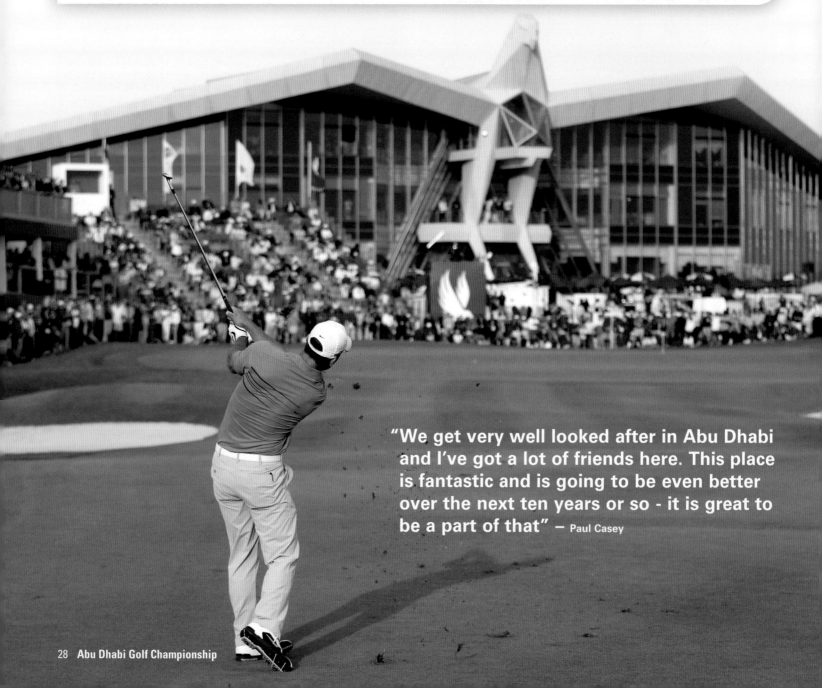

"We get very well looked after in Abu Dhabi and I've got a lot of friends here. This place is fantastic and is going to be even better over the next ten years or so - it is great to be a part of that" – Paul Casey

Abu Dhabi
travellers welcome

Padraig Harrington

Louis Oosthuizen

Martin Kaymer

Class and Composure

Paul Casey ensured his love affair with the Abu Dhabi Golf Championship continued to blossom when he captured the title for the second time in three years. In 2007, the Englishman won by one shot and that was the margin once again this time round, the 31 year old holding off the spirited challenges of defending champion Martin Kaymer of Germany and South Africa's Louis Oosthuizen, the latter particularly impressive with a flawless closing 64.

Kaymer spectacularly eagled the final hole for a 67 to join Oosthuizen on 20 under par 268 but Casey showed his class and composure to calmly par the final four

holes for a 70 and a winning total of 21 under par 267.

It was Casey's ninth European Tour International Schedule title – and the first since his success at the Abu Dhabi Golf Club in 2007 – and moved the Englishman from 30th to fifth place on The Race to Dubai. He also became the fifth most successful Englishman in the history of The European Tour – behind Nick Faldo with 30 wins, Mark James (18), Lee Westwood (18) and Howard Clark (11) – and proves marriage certainly agrees with him, having wed fiancée Jocelyn only a month earlier in America.

His Excellency Mubarak Al Mahairi, Director General of the Abu Dhabi Tourism Authority (third from the right seated) and Ahmed Hussein, Deputy Director General Tourism Operations of the ADTA (third from the left seated) are joined by leading players and sponsors at the CEO Round Table Dinner at the Emirates Palace Hotel

"To win a tournament on The European Tour is not something you do every day so it is a very special achievement and I am absolutely delighted"

— Alvaro Quiros

Commercial bank
Qatar Masters

PRESENTED BY
DOLPHIN ENERGY

COMMERCIALBANK QATAR MASTERS PRESENTED BY DOLPHIN ENERGY
Doha Golf Club
Doha, Qatar
January 22–25, 2009

EUROPEAN TOUR
RACE TO
DUBAI
2009

1	**ALVARO QUIROS**	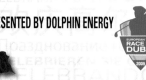	**69**	**67**	**64**	**69**	**269**	**-19**
2	Louis Oosthuizen		67	65	69	71	272	-16
	Henrik Stenson		66	72	66	68	272	-16
4	Damien McGrane		69	69	70	67	275	-13
5	Miguel Angel Jiménez		66	71	70	69	276	-12
	Maarten Lafeber		68	70	66	72	276	-12
7	Andrew Coltart		66	69	70	72	277	-11
	Simon Dyson		72	70	69	66	277	-11
	Gonzalo Fernandez-Castaño		69	72	67	69	277	-11
	Sergio Garcia		70	70	67	70	277	-11
	Chapchai Nirat		69	69	69	70	277	-11

Andrew Stevens, Group CEO of Commercialbank and Alvaro Quiros

Total Prize Fund €1,882,982   **First Prize** €314,400

Sergio García

Nick Dougherty

Miguel Angel Jiménez

Retief Goosen

Qatar's sporting vision
– winning the world's stage

Commercial bank
Qatar Masters ⑨⑨

PRESENTED BY

DOLPHIN دولفين
ENERGY للطاقة

January 28 - 31, 2010

Visionary leadership, supported by strong economic fundamentals and a sound financial system continue to place Qatar firmly on the world map as a leading business, financial, cultural and sporting destination. Commercialbank has played a part in the growth and prosperity of Qatar since 1975, financing the very infrastructure of the country and providing banking services that reach out to every aspect of Qatari life. More than just our home, Qatar is the source of our inspiration.

قطر مصدر إلهامنا
Inspired by Qatar
www.cbq.com.qa

البنك التجاري
Commercial bank

Andrew Coltart

Louis Oosthuizen

Worldwide Wonder

Alvaro Quiros continued his own worldwide golfing odyssey on The European Tour International Schedule when, as the only man with all four rounds in the 60s at the Doha Golf Club, he swept to a three shot victory in the Commercialbank Qatar Masters presented by Dolphin Energy.

The 26 year old Spaniard's two previous Tour successes had come in Africa in 2007 in the Alfred Dunhill Championship, and in Europe in 2008 in the Portugal Masters. Now, thanks to a combination of power play and precision, he added success in the Gulf to his burgeoning CV with a winning total of 19 under par 269.

Renowned for his big hitting, Quiros showed an adept touch on the greens too, especially during his sublime third round 64 which required him to use the putter on only 24 occasions.

Doha Golf Club specialist Henrik Stenson, the tournament winner in 2006, ensured his fifth straight top seven finish in the tournament with a closing round of 68 for 272 which saw the Swede share second place with South Africa's Louis Oosthuizen who had held the lead at the halfway stage after opening rounds of 67-65. Ireland's Damien McGrane carded a bogey free final round 67 to take fourth on 275.

Damien McGrane

Henrik Stenson

"When you look down the final leaderboard and see all the big names there – to have been able to beat a field of that strength and quality is very satisfying indeed" – Rory McIlroy

DUBAI DESERT CLASSIC
Emirates Golf Club (Majlis Course)
Dubai, UAE
January 29–February 1, 2009

1	RORY MCILROY		64	68	67	70	269	-19
2	Justin Rose		68	66	69	67	270	-18
3	Henrik Stenson		68	65	71	67	271	-17
4	Paul Casey		68	68	68	68	272	-16
	Robert Karlsson		65	71	71	65	272	-16
	Martin Kaymer		70	67	68	67	272	-16
7	Miguel Angel Jiménez		72	70	67	66	275	-13
	Louis Oosthuizen		68	65	68	74	275	-13
	Scott Strange		69	71	66	69	275	-13
	Anthony Wall		70	68	68	69	275	-13

Rory McIlroy and Sheikh Majid bin Mohammed bin Rashid Al Maktoum, Chairman of Dubai Culture and Arts Authority

Total Prize Fund €1,930,002   **First Prize** €323,514

Martin Kaymer

Teenage Kicks

Much has been written about Rory McIlroy in his relatively short professional golfing life and rightly so, for the teenager's achievements to date are hugely impressive.

At the end of the 2007 season he became the quickest Affiliate Member to secure his European Tour card – in just two events – and at the end of 2008 he became the youngest player to feature in the top 50 on the Official World Golf Ranking. The only thing missing for the 19 year old Northern Irishman was a victory but he put that right in considerable style in the Dubai Desert Classic.

In front from the moment he posted a first round 64, McIlroy was never headed as subsequent rounds of 68-67-70 gave him a wire to wire victory and a winning 19 under par total of 269. England's Justin Rose pushed him close in the final round with a 67 for 270 but McIlroy showed he possessed nerve as well as ability to get up and down from a bunker on the 72nd hole for a par five which confirmed his one shot success.

Earlier in the week, two time Major Champion Mark O'Meara claimed McIlroy was a better ball striker at 19 than Tiger Woods was. High praise indeed but, on this form, unquestionably merited.

Newly elected European Ryder Cup Captain Colin Montgomerie is congratulated by George O'Grady (left), The European Tour Chief Executive, and Ryder Cup Director Richard Hills

Justin Rose

Scott Strange

Robert Karlsson

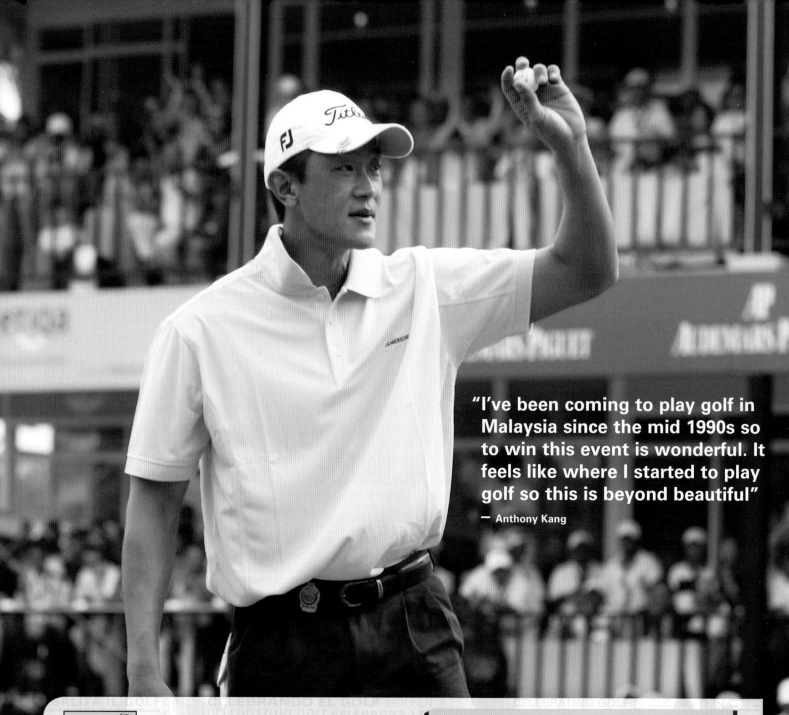

"I've been coming to play golf in Malaysia since the mid 1990s so to win this event is wonderful. It feels like where I started to play golf so this is beyond beautiful"

— Anthony Kang

MAYBANK MALAYSIAN OPEN
Saujana Golf and Country Club (Palm Course)
Kuala Lumpur, Malaysia
February 12–15, 2009

1	**ANTHONY KANG**		74	66	64	67	**271**	**-17**
2	David Horsey		71	68	69	64	272	-16
	Prayad Marksaeng		69	70	65	68	272	-16
	Jyoti Randhawa		71	69	66	66	272	-16
	Miles Tunnicliff		71	70	63	68	272	-16
6	Gareth Maybin		69	69	69	66	273	-15
7	Wen-Chong Liang		65	71	67	71	274	-14
	Alexander Noren		63	71	69	71	274	-14
	Louis Oosthuizen		70	71	68	65	274	-14
10	Adam Blyth		66	70	66	73	275	-13

L-R: Y.A.B Dato' Sri Mohd Najib Bin Tun Haji Abdul Razak, Prime Minister of Malaysia, Anthony Kang and Y.BHG Tan Sri Mohamed Basir Bin Ahmad, Chairman, Maybank

Total Prize Fund €1,564,312   **First Prize** €259,164

Gareth Maybin

Miles Tunnicliff

David Horsey

Jyoti Randhawa

King Kang

The fact that an American golfer called Anthony triumphed in the Maybank Malaysian Open did not come as a surprise to most golf observers; after all, US Ryder Cup star Anthony Kim, making his debut in the event, started the week as overwhelming favourite. However, it was not the World Number 11 who got his hands on the gleaming trophy at the end of the week, but his compatriot Anthony Kang who claimed an unexpected success.

The 36 year old – who came into the tournament at Number 318 on the Official World Golf Ranking – appeared an even more unlikely champion when he bogeyed

four of his last five holes to post an opening two over par 74 to share 102nd place at the end of the first round.

After that, however, Kang played like a man possessed. He dropped only one shot in his next three rounds – on the 15th in the final round – but he quickly made amends with a birdie four at the 580 yard 18th, a crucial thrust which moved him out of the logjam of four players – David Horsey, Prayad Marksaeng, Jyoti Randhawa and Miles Tunnicliff – tied for second on 16 under par 272 and gave him the winning total of 17 under par 271.

"It is pretty amazing what I have done – to win a European Tour event. It feels like I am in dreamland – hopefully nobody will wake me up" – Danny Lee

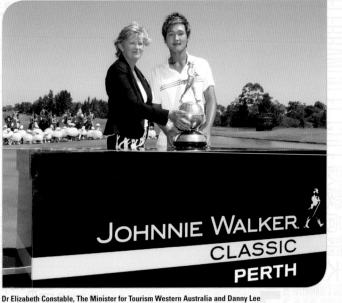

Dr Elizabeth Constable, The Minister for Tourism Western Australia and Danny Lee

Total Prize Fund €1,412,782

JOHNNIE WALKER CLASSIC
The Vines Resort and Country Club
Perth, Australia
February 19–22, 2009

1	**DANNY LEE (AM)**		67	68	69	67	271	-17
2	Felipe Aguilar		68	68	68	68	272	-16
	Hiroyuki Fujita		67	68	70	67	272	-16
	Ross McGowan		70	67	65	70	272	-16
5	John Bickerton		66	70	66	71	273	-15
	Raphaël Jacquelin		70	68	66	69	273	-15
7	Adam Blyth		68	68	71	67	274	-14
	Michael Sim		69	69	67	69	274	-14
	Lee Westwood		66	73	68	67	274	-14
10	Markus Brier		70	68	70	67	275	-13
	Paul Casey		71	68	70	66	275	-13
	Ignacio Garrido		67	68	70	70	275	-13
	Taichiro Kiyota		68	70	69	68	275	-13

Ross McGowan

Oh Danny Boy

It is not often that a golfer rewrites the record books with victory on The European Tour International Schedule but teenager Danny Lee did just that with a stunning triumph in the Johnnie Walker Classic.

Not only did he become only the second amateur in history – behind Spain's Pablo Martin in the 2007 Estoril Open de Portugal – to win a European Tour event, he also, at the age of 18 years and 213 days, became the youngest winner in Tour history, surpassing the previous record of South African Dale Hayes in the 1971 Spanish Open by 77 days.

Consistent opening rounds of 67-68-69 saw the young man, who was born of Korean parents but who moved to New Zealand at the age of eight, begin the final round in a share of third place, two shots behind the leading English duo of John Bickerton and Ross McGowan, but he accelerated to the title on the home stretch, birdieing the 13th and 14th as well as the 17th and 18th, to post a closing 67 for a 17 under par total of 271 and a one shot victory over Chile's Felipe Aguilar, Hiroyuki Fujita of Japan and McGowan.

Paul Casey

Raphaël Jacquelin

Felipe Aguilar

Paul Casey, Camilo Villegas, Anthony Kim, Greg Norman, Ian Poulter and Colin Montgomerie before the Pro-Celebrity event, organised to help the Victoria Bushfires Red Cross Appeal

"My key target for this year is to finish in the top 60 in The Race to Dubai and qualify for the Dubai World Championship – this has given me a good chance to do that" – Thongchai Jaidee

Thongchai Jaidee and His Excellence, Dr. Ing H. Fauzi Bowo, Governor of DKI Jakarta

ENJOY JAKARTA INDONESIA OPEN
New Kuta Golf Club
Bali, Indonesia
February 26–March 1, 2009

							Total	
1	**THONGCHAI JAIDEE**		71	69	67	69	276	-12
2	Simon Dyson		68	71	70	69	278	-10
	Alexander Noren		69	73	66	70	278	-10
	Steve Webster		69	69	72	68	278	-10
5	Richard Bland		72	71	66	70	279	-9
	Rafael Cabrera-Bello		71	72	71	65	279	-9
7	Simon Griffiths		70	70	69	71	280	-8
	Simon Khan		68	76	68	68	280	-8
	Jyoti Randhawa		74	70	66	70	280	-8
10	Jason Knutzon		72	70	70	69	281	-7
	Seung-yul Noh		69	76	70	66	281	-7

Total Prize Fund €981,417   **First Prize** €163,867

Alex Noren

Steve Webster

Richard Bland

Simon Dyson

Flying High

In recent years, Thai golfers such as Prayad Marksaeng, Chapchai Nirat and Thaworn Wiratchant have all become prominent on The European Tour International Schedule with, indeed, Nirat and Wiratchant featuring in the winners' circle.

However they all recognise the part played in their success by the doyen of Thai golf, Thongchai Jaidee, who blazed a trail for their country and who, as he showed in the Enjoy Jakarta Indonesia Open, is still more than capable of competing at the sharp end of tournament golf.

The 39 year old former paratrooper in the Royal Thai Army pulled the ripcord to inflate his challenge with a fine third round 67 which gave him a one shot lead over Sweden's Alexander Noren going into the final round.

Four birdies in his first seven holes on Sunday gave Jaidee a four shot lead before a momentary wobble allowed England's Steve Webster to close the gap to one. But Jaidee held his nerve and a birdie four on the 16th hole saw him complete a final round 69 for a 12 under par total of 276 and a two shot victory over Simon Dyson, Noren and Webster, a victory which helped him rise to 16th place in The Race to Dubai.

WGC - ACCENTURE MATCH PLAY
Ritz-Carlton Golf Club
Dove Mountain, Marana, Arizona, USA
February 25–March 1, 2009

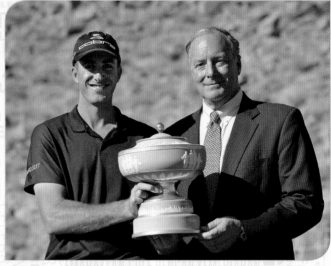

Geoff Ogilvy and William Green, Chairman and CEO, Accenture

CHAMPION	GEOFF OGILVY	
Runner-Up	Paul Casey	
Third	Stewart Cink	
Fourth	Ross Fisher	

Final: Geoff Ogilvy beat Paul Casey 4 and 3
Consolation Final: Stewart Cink beat Ross Fisher 1 hole

Total Prize Fund €6,685,882   **First Prize** €1,101,204

"I played better and better during the week - in fact every round I seemed to improve. It doesn't often happen that way in golf so it was nice to have that progression" – Geoff Ogilvy

Showpiece Showdown

Geoff Ogilvy's fantastic victory in the World Golf Championships – Accenture Match Play capped not only a wonderful week for the Australian himself in Arizona, but also for The European Tour Membership as a whole.

The 31 year old from Adelaide, the winner of the event also in 2006, beat England's Paul Casey 4 and 3 in the 36 hole final – the first time in the 11 year history of the event that the showpiece showdown had featured two European Tour Members.

Ogilvy was three up at lunch and excellent play saw him double that advantage by the ninth hole of the afternoon. Casey battled to win the 11th and 13th, but a half in par four was enough for the Australian to take the title on the 15th green.

The final was the icing on the cake of a memorable five days in the desert which began with a record 47 European Tour Members in the starting field of 64 with five – Ernie Els, Ross Fisher, Rory McIlroy, Casey and Ogilvy – in the last eight.

All made significant moves in The Race to Dubai with, naturally, Ogilvy making the biggest strides. He moved from 18th to Number One with Casey moving from eighth to second place. The duo also graduated to World Number Four and 13 respectively.

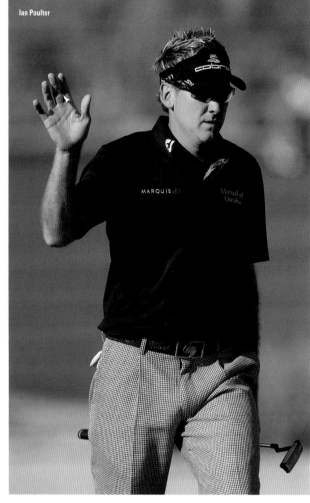
Ian Poulter

Ross Fisher and Paul Casey

Ernie Els

WGC - CA CHAMPIONSHIP
Doral Golf Resort and Spa
Doral, Florida, USA
March 12–15, 2009

1	**PHIL MICKELSON**		**65**	**66**	**69**	**69**	**269**	**-19**
2	Nick Watney		66	67	67	70	270	-18
3	Jim Furyk		68	68	69	67	272	-16
4	Jeev Milkha Singh		65	71	68	70	274	-14
5	Camilo Villegas		67	68	69	71	275	-13
	Oliver Wilson		67	70	72	66	275	-13
7	Thomas Aiken		74	66	71	65	276	-12
	Søren Kjeldsen		70	66	69	71	276	-12
9	Justin Leonard		69	69	68	71	277	-11
	Rodney Pampling		66	69	71	71	277	-11
	Kenny Perry		70	64	71	72	277	-11
	Tiger Woods		71	70	68	68	277	-11

John Swainson, CEO of CA and Phil Mickelson

Total Prize Fund €6,681,337   **First Prize** €1,105,005

"I love the process of competing, of being in the final group tied for the lead, feeling the pressure and the intensity and how important each shot is" — Phil Mickelson

Camilo Villegas

Søren Kjeldsen

Oliver Wilson

Jeev Milkha Singh

Grit and Determination

Phil Mickelson showed grit and determination alongside his golfing ability with a battling one shot victory over fellow countryman Nick Watney in the World Golf Championships – CA Championship.

The left hander had spent most of Saturday evening in the emergency room of a local Miami hospital suffering from heat exhaustion and dehydration and went into the final round having been given two bags of an IV solution.

However, any hopes Watney harboured that Mickelson was going to be a pushover were banished in an extraordinary front nine which began with the two main protagonists locked together on 16 under

par before the lead changed hands three times in a see-saw front nine tussle which closely resembled a match play duel at times.

Mickelson edged in front again as the pair turned for home and produced par figures at each of the closing seven holes to hold off his young compatriot who faced a 30 foot putt on the final green to send the championship into extra holes, but left it agonisingly short. At 19 under par 269, it was Mickelson's first victory in a WGC event in his 27th attempt and moved him back to Number Two on the Official World Golf Ranking.

MADEIRA ISLANDS OPEN BPI - PORTUGAL
Porto Santo Golfe
Madeira, Portugal
March 19–22, 2009

1	**TANO GOYA**		68	68	69	73	**278**	**-6**
2	Callum Macaulay		74	74	67	64	279	-5
3	Wil Besseling		69	72	70	69	280	-4
	Damien McGrane		66	72	70	72	280	-4
5	Anthony Wall		72	69	73	67	281	-3
6	Michael Hoey		69	66	75	72	282	-2
7	Thomas Aiken		72	69	71	71	283	-1
	Joakim Haeggman		66	70	75	72	283	-1
9	David Drysdale		72	72	71	69	284	0
	Jan-Are Larsen		71	71	76	66	284	0

José Carlos Agrellos, Executive Director of BPI and Tano Goya

Total Prize Fund €704,182 **First Prize** €116,660

> "Just over a year ago I was thinking
> how much I would love to play on The
> European Tour and here I am now having
> won on it – it is a truly amazing feeling"

— Tano Goya

Joao Cunha e Silva, Vice President of the Regional Government of Madeira, heads the party which unveiled a plaque to honour Seve Ballesteros, the designer of the course at Porto Santo Golfe

Wil Besseling

Damien McGrane

Fantasy Island

Tano Goya survived a late scare and an amazing birdie burst by Scotland's Callum Macaulay to win a European Tour title in just his sixth attempt. The 20 year old from Cordoba, a graduate from last season's European Challenge Tour, captured the Madeira Islands Open BPI – Portugal by a solitary shot with a closing 73 for a six under par total of 278.

The Argentine's success helped him move 100 places in The Race to Dubai – from 150th to 50th place – and he immediately targeted a place in the inaugural Dubai World Championship in November as his main goal. What had begun the season as fantasy, now had a chance of being reality.

Northern Irishman Michael Hoey held the lead at the halfway stage but when he fell back with a third round 75, Goya's 69 saw him move into pole position. Ten shots behind going into Sunday, Macaulay barely merited a glance from Goya but his stunning final round 64 – which featured a back nine of 28 – changed all that, the Scot setting the clubhouse target of five under par 279. Goya was on course to beat that before a double bogey six at the 16th gave Macaulay a glimmer of hope. But two closing pars from the Argentine ended all doubt as to the destination of the trophy.

Joakim Haeggman

OPEN DE ANDALUCIA DE GOLF 09
Real Club de Golf de Sevilla
Seville, Spain
March 26-29, 2009

1	**SØREN KJELDSEN**		68	72	62	72	**274**	**-14**
2	David Drysdale		70	67	66	74	277	-11
3	Francesco Molinari		72	68	68	70	278	-10
	Graeme Storm		70	66	73	69	278	-10
5	Alastair Forsyth		74	64	68	73	279	-9
6	Andrew Coltart		68	73	69	70	280	-8
	Rhys Davies		75	67	68	70	280	-8
	Marcel Siem		68	67	73	72	280	-8
9	Thomas Aiken		70	72	69	70	281	-7
	John E Morgan		70	73	69	69	281	-7

www.opendeandalucia.com

L-R: Javier Subijana, Director General de Valle Romano, Søren Kjeldsen and Manuel Jiménez Barrios, Secretario General para el Deporte, Junta de Andalucía

Total Prize Fund €998,170   **First Prize** €166,660

"The last few months have been great. There is no doubt I am more comfortable now and my game is in the best shape it has ever been – I am definitely moving in the right direction" – Søren Kjeldsen

Alastair Forsyth

Spanish Ayes

It is a fair bet that when asked to choose a holiday destination, Søren Kjeldsen will plump for Andalucia; after all, the region of Spain has been very good to the 33 year old Dane of late.

Just over four months before he arrived for the Open de Andalucia de Golf 09, the little man from Aalborg had stood tall at Club de Golf Valderrama to win the 21st and final Volvo Masters. Now here he was in Seville, triumphing again, his victory thanks largely to a stunning third round 62 which set a new course record on the José Maria Olazábal-designed layout.

In a share of 16th place at halfway, Kjeldsen had done little to grab the headlines in the early part of the week, most of those reserved for Colin Montgomerie who was making his 500th European Tour appearance. But the 62 changed all that and gave him a one shot lead over Montgomerie's fellow Scot, David Drysdale.

The two leading protagonists fought a thrilling battle over the closing stages of the final round with Kjeldsen holing crucial 20 footers on both the 16th and 17th for a par five and a birdie two respectively. It forced Drysdale to push for a birdie at the last but when he found the water, his challenge was over.

Miguel Angel Jiménez

David Drysdale

Colin Montgomerie was presented with an engraved Ice Bucket and a jeroboam of Moët & Chandon champagne to mark his 500th European Tour appearance

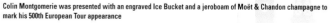

ESTORIL OPEN DE PORTUGAL

Oitavos Dunes
Cascais, Portugal
April 2-5, 2009

L-R: Duate Nobre Guedes, President of Costa do Estoril Tourism Board,
Michael Hoey and Manuel Agrellos, President of the Portuguese Golf Federation

1	**MICHAEL HOEY**		66	76	69	66	**277**	**-7**
2	Gonzalo Fernandez-Castaño		70	72	68	67	277	-7
3	Francesco Molinari		71	71	68	68	278	-6
4	Paul Broadhurst		71	68	67	73	279	-5
	Jamie Donaldson		71	69	67	72	279	-5
	Mikael Lundberg		70	72	67	70	279	-5
7	Grégory Bourdy		69	73	69	69	280	-4
	Alastair Forsyth		67	73	69	71	280	-4
	Paul Lawrie		71	69	68	72	280	-4
	David Lynn		69	73	65	73	280	-4
	Steve Webster		68	72	71	69	280	-4

Total Prize Fund €1,261,205   **First Prize** €208,330

"This means absolutely everything to me. I've dreamt about playing on Tour, never mind winning, so this really is a life changing moment. This is what you practise for" — Michael Hoey

Ross McGowan

Paul Broadhurst

Jamie Donaldson

Gonzalo Fernandez-Castaño

Perfect Return

For the fifth time on The 2009 European Tour International Schedule, extra holes were required to find a champion and, after the dust had settled, Irish eyes were smiling as Ulsterman Michael Hoey overcame Spaniard Gonzalo Fernandez-Castaño to win the Estoril Open de Portugal.

It was the perfect return to the country for the 30 year old who had led the Madeira Islands Open BPI – Portugal after two rounds two weeks previously before slipping back. This time, however, there was no such prominence at halfway; a second round 76 seeing him enter the weekend action outside the top 20. A third

round 69 moved him in the right direction, before a superb closing 66 – allied to Fernandez-Castaño's 67 – saw the pair both emerge from the chasing pack to finish tied on seven under par 277 at the end of regulation play.

Two trips to the 18th failed to separate the duo before the end came at the demanding 475 yard, par four 17th. Both players missed the green with their approach shots leaving Fernandez-Castaño to play first. The Spaniard chipped to 12 feet while Hoey, restricted by a tree branch, did well to pitch to six. When Fernandez-Castaño's par putt stayed above ground, Hoey knew what he had to do – and he did.

MASTERS TOURNAMENT
Augusta National Golf Club
Augusta, Georgia, USA
April 9-12, 2009

1	**ANGEL CABRERA**		68	68	69	71	276	-12
2	Chad Campbell		65	70	72	69	276	-12
	Kenny Perry		68	67	70	71	276	-12
4	Shingo Katayama		67	73	70	68	278	-10
5	Phil Mickelson		73	68	71	67	279	-9
6	Steve Flesch		71	74	68	67	280	-8
	John Merrick		68	74	72	66	280	-8
	Steve Stricker		72	69	68	71	280	-8
	Tiger Woods		70	72	70	68	280	-8
10	Jim Furyk		66	74	68	73	281	-7
	Hunter Mahan		66	75	71	69	281	-7
	Sean O'Hair		68	76	68	69	281	-7

Trevor Immelman, the 2008 Masters Tournament Champion, presents the Green Jacket to Angel Cabrera

Total Prize Fund €5,647,429   **First Prize** €1,005,748

"This is the Masters and a lot of magical things happen here. Two years ago, the US Open took me a little bit by surprise – for this win I was more prepared and more aware of things" – Angel Cabrera

Master Magician

Angel Cabrera brought his home town of Cordoba to a standstill when he returned home with the US Open Championship trophy in 2007, with the party going on for two days. In many ways, the hangover for the 39 year old Argentine lasted almost two years, until he recognised his destiny resting among the blooming azaleas and magnolias which adorned a truly special Masters Tournament.

Ian Poulter

Rory McIlroy

Cabrera arrived at Augusta National without a single top five finish in over 12 months, a preposterous record for someone laden with his talent. The bookmakers had him at 125/1 to win. How could he turn round such an indifferent run of form and remember the player within? Thus do the great players distinguish themselves, drawing inspiration from their surroundings and belief in their fate.

Is there a more heart-warming story in golf than Cabrera's rise from grinding poverty to become a living embodiment of the American dream? Even the briefest recap of his journey makes the jaw go slack: the boy who became a caddie at the age of just ten because there was no other choice; who purportedly turned up for his first job wearing no shoes. From such humble surroundings he became one of the world's purest ball strikers, and now he has a Green Jacket and Honorary Membership of one of the most exclusive golf clubs in the world. They make movies about such things, don't they?

For such a proud nation of golfers as Argentina, this triumph must have felt like closure, two generations on from the scorecard error of their great patriarch, Roberto de Vicenzo, who signed for a 66 rather than the 65 he actually shot in the final round, thus depriving him of a play-off against Bob Goalby in 1968.

Now here was Cabrera, with destiny inevitably declaring that he should win by the play-off route so cruelly denied his compatriot. Certainly it was almost as if some guiding force was showing its hand as Cabrera, two strokes adrift of the luckless Kenny Perry with two holes to play, was given a reprieve following successive bogeys from his opponent. If that was not enough, there was the

drama of the first play-off hole, which featured another American, Chad Campbell, alongside Cabrera and Perry. What escape could there possibly be for the Argentine following a drive into the trees while his two opponents were in the middle of the fairway?

Once more Cabrera found a way, with the stoic refusal to give in to circumstance that is the preserve of so many Major winners. Then, at the second play-off hole, he showed his class, the difficult par four tenth yielding to two quality blows to finally defeat Perry, after Campbell had dropped out a hole earlier.

It was the first three man play-off since 1987, and here was more evidence for believers in destiny. On that Sunday, 22 years earlier, Cabrera's great hero Seve Ballesteros had walked back up the very same hill at the tenth with tears streaming down his face after losing out to Greg Norman and, ultimately, Larry Mize. Now a week that had begun with former winners saying prayers for the absent Spaniard at the Champions' Dinner, ended with his protégé winning a Green Jacket on that fateful play-off hole.

Thus did one of the great Masters Tournaments come to its momentous, fairytale conclusion. So much for a tournament that had lost its roars, its magic. Amazing what a bit of luck with the weather and a bit of tweaking from the organisers with regard to tees, pin positions, and moisture in the greens can bring about.

What was your favourite bit? Was it Rory McIlroy, surely a future winner, playing all four rounds on his debut and indeed the final nine holes on Sunday in just 31 blows? Was it the sight of so many records falling, right from the moment

Ross Fisher

Henrik Stenson

Sandy Lyle

EVERY IMPROVEMENT COUNTS.
BECAUSE EVERY SHOT COUNTS.

The Titleist Pro V1 and Pro V1x

Your golf ball is the only piece of equipment you use for every shot. And now we've made the game's most technologically advanced, best performing golf balls even better. The Pro V1® delivers more distance and more spin for better control and the Pro V1x™ delivers longer distance. Both more durable than ever. We're always improving our game, so you can improve yours. To learn more, go to titleist.co.uk

Justin Rose

Campbell became the first man in Masters Tournament history to begin the event with five straight birdies? Was it the almost unbroken sunshine that bathed these sacred acres in such a wondrous light for almost the entire 72 holes?

Many people, one suspects, would plump for the final round pairing of Phil Mickelson and Tiger Woods for the first time in a Major. They set the tone for the last round with a truly memorable display of shot making from the former and typical doggedness from the latter. Either could have won if they could have maintained their momentum for 18 rather than 16 holes, but what drama they brought to the occasion, what excitement for three and a half of the four hours they were paired.

However, it is something else that many will always recall; namely the exemplary sportsmanship that unfolded over the tense closing holes between Cabrera and Perry.

It began with Cabrera saluting the sterling tee shot that Perry played to the short 16th hole that finished stone dead – never mind that it looked to have cost the South American the tournament.

Then there was the American returning the gesture after Cabrera's remarkable par four at the first play-off hole, applauding openly even though the holed eight foot putt meant the contest went on rather than ending there with the culmination of his own personal dream, namely becoming the oldest player in history to win a Major Championship.

In these moments we are given reminders why we follow this sport rather than a hundred others. With such gestures we learn why golfers are held up as paragons by sportsmen in virtually every other field of endeavour.

Derek Lawrenson
Daily Mail

Gary Player

Tiger Woods and Phil Mickelson

VOLVO

VOLVO CHINA OPEN
Beijing CBD International Golf Club
Beijing, China
April 16–19, 2009

1	**SCOTT STRANGE**		**70**	**73**	**69**	**68**	**280**	**-8**
2	Gonzalo Fernandez-Castaño		71	70	68	72	281	-7
3	Mark Brown		71	77	65	69	282	-6
	Richard Finch		71	71	66	74	282	-6
	Ashley Hall		75	71	65	71	282	-6
6	David Dixon		72	73	67	71	283	-5
	Stephen Dodd		74	71	70	68	283	-5
8	Markus Brier		67	73	71	73	284	-4
	Paul McGinley		74	67	75	68	284	-4
	Chapchai Nirat		69	71	72	72	284	-4

Per Ericsson, President & CEO, Volvo Event Management and Scott Strange

Total Prize Fund €1,662,349   **First Prize** €275,813

"This is the first time in my career that I have won when not leading from the front which shows I have another string to my bow. To come from four shots back was pretty exciting" — Scott Strange

Gonzalo Fernandez-Castaño

Mark Brown

On the Rails

In his Asian Tour victories in the Philippines and Myanmar and also in his emotional triumph in last year's Celtic Manor Wales Open – a victory achieved a week before he lost his sister Natalie to cancer – Scott Strange had always led from the front in the final round. Indeed, in Myanmar and Wales he won wire-to-wire. In the Volvo China Open, however, he discovered another facet to his game when he came from behind on the last day to succeed.

Going into Sunday's action four shots adrift of England's Richard Finch and deep in the chasing pack, Strange was not amongst

the favourites, but changed all that with a superb closing four under par 68 which saw the 32 year old Australian come up on the rails to set the clubhouse target of eight under par 280.

With leader Finch slipping back to tie for third place with Mark Brown and Ashley Hall, it was left to the Englishman's playing partner, Gonzalo Fernandez-Castaño, to try and match Strange's tally. The Spaniard needed an eagle three at the final hole to do so and although he managed a creditable birdie four on the 564 yard hole, it was not enough to force a play-off.

Richard Finch

BALLANTINE'S CHAMPIONSHIP
Pinx Golf Club
Jeju Island, South Korea
April 23–26, 2009

1	**THONGCHAI JAIDEE**		**66**	**71**	**77**	**70**	**284**	**-4**
2	Gonzalo Fernandez-Castaño		65	74	76	69	284	-4
	Sung-hoon Kang		69	71	76	68	284	-4
4	Seve Benson		69	70	78	69	286	-2
	Rafael Cabrera-Bello		68	72	76	70	286	-2
	Robert-Jan Derksen		66	69	75	76	286	-2
	Ernie Els		68	74	73	71	286	-2
8	Peter Lawrie		70	75	76	66	287	-1
	Mardan Mamat		69	70	77	71	287	-1
	Danny Willett		69	76	73	69	287	-1

Christian Porta, Chairman and CEO of Chivas and Thongchai Jaidee

Total Prize Fund €2,112,582   **First Prize** €350,000

"I phoned home every day and one night my son said to me: 'Daddy, I want you to bring the trophy home.' I am so happy to be able to do that for him" – Thongchai Jaidee

Rafael Cabrera-Bello and Gonzalo Fernandez-Castaño

Robert-Jan Derksen

John Paramor, European Tour Chief Referee

Father's Day

As a former paratrooper in the Royal Thai Army, Thongchai Jaidee knows all about gauging the strength and direction of the wind, qualities which stood him in good stead as he claimed the Ballantine's Championship in some of the toughest conditions ever encountered at a European Tour event.

Jeju Island may be renowned for its winds but the severity of the gusts on Saturday in particular, along with the plummeting temperatures saw only one player out of 74 – François Delamontagne – break the par of 72.

Jaidee battled to a 77 to share third place going into the final day, four shots adrift of leader Robert-Jan Derksen, but when the Dutchman slipped back, Jaidee seized his chance and a closing 70 saw him finish level with Gonzalo Fernandez-Castaño of Spain and Korea's Kang Sung-hoon on four under par 284.

Second to Michael Hoey in Portugal and Scott Strange in China in his previous two outings, Fernandez-Castaño was desperate to avoid an unwanted hat-trick, but so it transpired as Jaidee took the glory at the first time of asking on the 18th, a stunning eight iron approach to four feet setting up a winning birdie three.

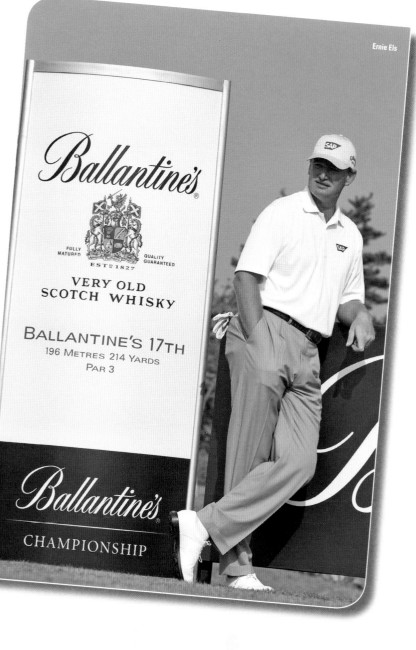
Ernie Els

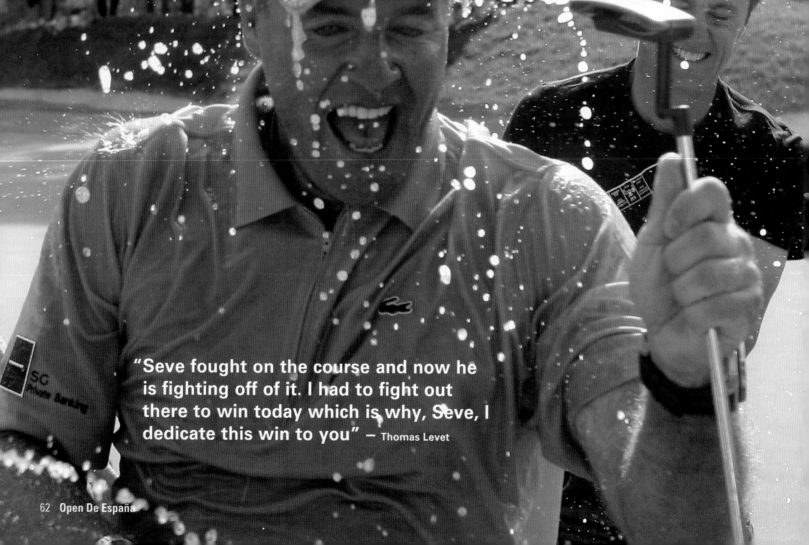

OPEN DE ESPAÑA
PGA Golf Catalunya (Stadium Course)
Girona, Spain
April 30-May 3, 2009

1	**THOMAS LEVET**		64	67	71	68	270	-18
2	Fabrizio Zanotti		71	70	66	65	272	-16
3	Thomas Björn		70	67	71	66	274	-14
	Peter Lawrie		68	66	71	69	274	-14
5	Charl Schwartzel		67	73	69	69	278	-10
6	Rafael Cabrera-Bello		70	67	74	68	279	-9
	Marcel Siem		67	70	72	70	279	-9
8	Grégory Bourdy		71	71	72	66	280	-8
	David Horsey		72	70	72	66	280	-8
	José Manuel Lara		65	73	71	71	280	-8

Thomas Levet and Gonzaga Escauriaza, President of the Royal Spanish Golf Federation

Total Prize Fund €2,000,000   **First Prize** €333,330

"Seve fought on the course and now he is fighting off of it. I had to fight out there to win today which is why, Seve, I dedicate this win to you" — Thomas Levet

Søren Hansen

French Resistance

Thomas Levet became the most successful Frenchman in the history of The European Tour with this, his fifth triumph, and immediately dedicated the victory on Spanish soil to the nation's favourite golfer, Seve Ballesteros, and his continuing fight to recover from brain surgery.

Levet revealed it was his long-time friendship with players such as Seve and José Maria Olazábal that had encouraged him to add Spanish to his impressive portfolio of languages and it was particularly appreciated by the crowds around the prizegiving ceremony that the new champion thanked them all in their native tongue.

One shot behind Søren Hansen after the first round, Levet took control of the tournament at the halfway stage with a second round 67. The 40 year old Parisian still led come Saturday night but fell behind in the early stages of the final round as England's Stuart Davis started with three straight birdies. Levet battled back to regain the advantage as Davis fell back only for the next wave of attack to come from Paraguay's Fabrizio Zanotti, in the penultimate group, who closed with a best of the day 65. Showing continued resilience however, Levet coolly birdied both the 15th and 17th to ensure his two shot victory.

Thomas Björn

Miguel Angel Jiménez

"When Cabrera won the Masters, every Argentine player changed the way they think. He has lots of confidence and I have learned that – it helps me to think better on the course" – Daniel Vancsik

BMW

The Ultimate Driving Machine

bmw-golfsport.com
bmw.co.uk

BMW ITALIAN OPEN
Royal Park I Roveri
Turin, Italy
May 7-10, 2009

EUROPEAN TOUR
RACE TO DUBAI
2009

1	**DANIEL VANCSIK**		68	65	69	65	**267**	**-17**
2	John Daly		69	69	69	66	273	-11
	Raphaël Jacquelin		67	70	68	68	273	-11
	Robert Rock		72	65	68	68	273	-11
5	Thomas Aiken		68	70	66	70	274	-10
6	Thomas Björn		71	67	68	69	275	-9
	Francesco Molinari		68	69	73	65	275	-9
8	Julien Clément		70	67	69	70	276	-8
	Robert Dinwiddie		72	67	68	69	276	-8
	Alastair Forsyth		73	68	67	68	276	-8
	Roope Kakko		71	64	68	73	276	-8
	Gareth Maybin		64	70	70	72	276	-8
	Peter O'Malley		74	68	64	70	276	-8

BMW Italian Open 2009

Andrea Castronovo, Presidente e AD BMW Group Italia and Daniel Vancsik

Total Prize Fund €1,297,620   **First Prize** €216,660

Feast or Famine

Roope Kakko

Raphaël Jacquelin

When he wins on The European Tour, he certainly does it in style as Daniel Vancsik proved once again with a majestic triumph in the BMW Italian Open. In his maiden Tour triumph in the 2007 Madeira Islands Open BPI, he won by seven shots, while this time the margin was six following a superb best of day final round 65 for a winning total of 17 under par 267.

Beginning Sunday with a slender one stroke advantage, the 32 year old Argentine quickly stamped his authority on proceedings, birdieing four of the first six holes to be out in 32, before ending the tournament as a contest with three further birdies in the first five holes of the inward half. Distant second place was shared between Raphaël Jacquelin, Robert Rock and a resurgent John Daly.

It is certainly a feast or a famine on Tour for Vancsik, who credited fellow countryman Angel Cabrera as the inspiration for his latest success. His victory in Madeira came on his 50th start, with the previous 49 not containing a single top ten, while his win in Italy came over a year after he recorded his previous top ten finish, in the Maybank Malaysian Open in March 2008.

John Daly

IRISH OPEN

THE 3 IRISH OPEN
County Louth Golf Club
Baltray, Drogheda, Ireland
May 14–17, 2009

L-R: Martin Cullen, Minister for Arts, Sports and Tourism TD, An Taoiseach Brian Cowen TD, Shane Lowry and Robert Finnegan, CEO of 3

1	**SHANE LOWRY (AM)**		67	62	71	71	271	-17
2	Robert Rock		66	65	69	71	271	-17
3	Johan Edfors		64	70	68	71	273	-15
4	Nick Dougherty		66	67	73	69	275	-13
	Marc Warren		67	69	71	68	275	-13
6	Alastair Forsyth		67	68	71	70	276	-12
7	Roope Kakko		66	67	76	69	278	-10
8	Thomas Levet		67	66	73	73	279	-9
	Brett Rumford		73	66	72	68	279	-9
10	Richard Bland		71	68	71	70	280	-8
	Anthony Wall		72	68	71	69	280	-8
	Chris Wood		69	67	76	68	280	-8

Total Prize Fund €3,000,000

"I cannot describe what I'm feeling – shocked more than anything else. I would have been happy just to make the cut but after the 62, I thought I could win. And now I have. Unbelievable"

— Shane Lowry

Johan Edfors

Robert Rock

Colin Montgomerie

Wherever Ireland takes you, you'll never be more than a chip and run from a great golf course.

We're all for detours. They're what make a holiday great. But you won't have to go out of your way to play a round of golf in Ireland, thanks to our four hundred courses. And with green fees from as little as £24, you won't have to go miles outside your budget either. For more information on golfing in Ireland visit **www.discoverireland.com/golf or freephone 0800 294 2009.**

SOLHEIM CUP

EUROPE · USA
KILLEEN CASTLE
IRELAND
2011

Go where Ireland *takes you*

Christy O'Connor (left) is congratulated by Sean McKeon, Captain of The Royal Dublin Golf Club, on the news he is to be inducted into the World Golf Hall of Fame

Marc Warren

Alastair Forsyth

Amateur Dramatics

Events on The European Tour do not often enter the realms of fairytale but The 3 Irish Open certainly did thanks to a sensational victory by Irish amateur Shane Lowry. The 22 year old became only the third amateur in history – following Pablo Martin and Danny Lee – to win a Tour event but the first to do so on home soil amongst tumultuous scenes of celebration.

However, what agonies the son of renowned Gaelic footballer Brendan Lowry had to go through before getting the better of England's Robert Rock in a play-off. Having raised his cap to the galleries as he walked onto the 72nd green to face a three

foot putt to win, the young man – who had carded a 62 in the second round to take control of the tournament – was soon covering his face with it when he pulled the putt wide.

Rock then missed a ten footer at the first play-off hole before the second was shared in birdie four. On the third trip to the 18th green moments later, Lowry's tap in for a par five was enough after Rock pitched over the green on his way to a bogey six. Rock had the €500,000 winner's cheque as consolation. For Lowry, there was simply elation.

Above Paul Lawrie won an Audi A5 Cabriolet for his hole in one at the 17th hole in round two, and received the keys from John Hayes, Deputy Director of Audi Ireland

ROLEX

BMW PGA

Simply Sensational

BMW PGA CHAMPIONSHIP
Wentworth Club (West Course)
Surrey, England
May 21-24, 2009

1	PAUL CASEY		69	67	67	68	271	-17
2	Ross Fisher		68	73	67	64	272	-16
3	Søren Kjeldsen		69	69	68	69	275	-13
4	Stephen Dodd		71	68	70	67	276	-12
5	Rory McIlroy		72	70	65	71	278	-10
6	Ben Curtis		69	70	73	67	279	-9
	Charl Schwartzel		68	72	68	71	279	-9
	Anthony Wall		67	71	72	69	279	-9
9	Thomas Levet		70	71	68	71	280	-8
10	Thomas Aiken		72	67	74	68	281	-7

L-R: Ian Robertson, Member of the Board, Sales and Marketing BMW Group, Paul Casey and George O'Grady, Chief Executive of The European Tour

Total Prize Fund €4,553,916   **First Prize** €750,000

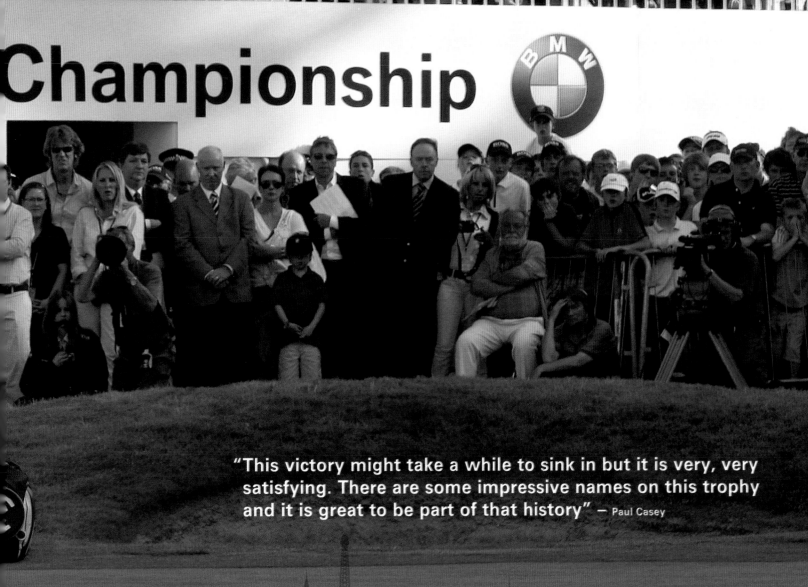

Championship

"This victory might take a while to sink in but it is very, very satisfying. There are some impressive names on this trophy and it is great to be part of that history" — Paul Casey

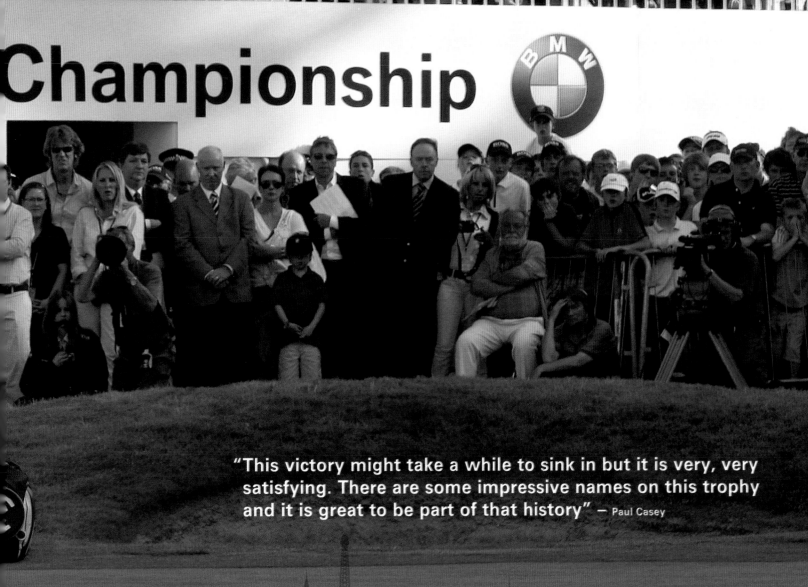

71

Moscow to Surrey is a giant step for any man and the young Russian security guard on duty outside the Media Centre during the BMW PGA Championship did not try to disguise his delight at being in the centre of things during what turned out to be a blistering week in more ways than one.

"It is," he said when asked how he felt about his new surroundings, "Bloody terrific." He was absolutely spot on. This really was one bloody terrific week. Blessed by weather good enough to pass as summer anywhere in this chaotic world, Wentworth Club sparkled like the jewel it is while the West Course offered visual delight and serious challenge in equal measure. When it is like this, there is simply no better place to be.

This is a thought that Paul Casey shares. The Englishman grew up just down the road, was first brought to Wentworth by his father when he was nine years old and can still vividly recall his delight at hearing the 'fizz' of drives by the likes of Seve Ballesteros, Nick Faldo, Sandy Lyle and Ian Woosnam.

By nine, Casey knew what he wanted to do in life. Ironically, as it happened, it was not to be a professional golfer. Instead he listed tennis as his first love, a devotion that was switched when he failed to gain a tennis scholarship. By the age of ten, he was hunting a scholarship again, this time in golf, and this time he was successful thanks to his local Foxhills Golf Club. Wimbledon's loss has undoubtedly been Wentworth's gain.

"That changed everything for me," he said as he cradled the gleaming trophy, his eager eyes flicking across the impressive list of past champions inscribed thereon. "I had free membership, free tuition, everything I needed. There are some truly great golf clubs in this part of the world but my parents couldn't afford to join any of them. Without that Foxhills scholarship who knows where I'd be now."

No doubting, however, where precisely he was after this fabulous victory – third on the Official World Golf Ranking, a

seriously reassuring upwards surge for a player who was worried about holding on to his top 50 position just a few months earlier. The difference? Victories in the Abu Dhabi Golf Championship, the Shell Houston Open and now the BMW PGA Championship. The reason? More self-belief, harder work with coach Peter Kostis, and probably a smidgeon more luck.

Nothing lucky, however, about his response to another local lad's last round 64, the undisputed round of the week from Ross Fisher. At 16 under par 272, the 28 year old from Ascot had set a serious target. Casey's response however – three birdies in the final four holes to win by a shot – underlined his tenacity as well as his quality. His birdie four from the greenside bunker at the last, in particular, offered compelling evidence of proper nerve.

But then this had been a championship worthy of the description, a week embroidered with much worth recalling. It started, as always, with The European Tour's Annual Dinner. Staged in Wentworth Club's dazzling ballroom, the occasion was graced with some of the top names in golf. They included Masters Tournament Champion Angel Cabrera, who received rapturous applause from the audience following a glowing tribute delivered by José Maria Olazábal, The Players Championship victor Henrik Stenson, and Ireland's own Open Championship and US PGA Championship hero Padraig Harrington who collected the inaugural European Tour Players' Player of the Year Award from his peers.

Brian Whitcomb, Honorary President of the PGA of America, gave a Stateside view of affairs while Rhodri Morgan, First Minister for Wales, spoke of his country's excitement as The 2010 Ryder Cup gets

Rory McIlroy

Ben Curtis

Anders Hansen

Charl Schwartzel

Ross Fisher

Genworth Financial

Above José Maria Olazábal (centre) became only the second Spaniard after Seve Ballesteros to be elected to the World Golf Hall of Fame. Jack Peter (left) Senior Vice President and Chief Operating Officer of the World Golf Hall of Fame, and George O'Grady (right) Chief Executive of The European Tour joined together to congratulate Olazábal on the honour

THE FIRST OF ITS KIND.

Even by BMW's standards the new 5 Series Gran Turismo is unique. Its revolutionary design combines elegance, versatility, space and, of course, dynamic yet efficient driving performance. Inside, the cabin is luxuriously appointed with reclining rear seats and a panoramic sunroof that lets passengers relax as the world flies by. After all, if you want to travel – it always pays to go first class. Contact your BMW Dealer or visit bmw.co.uk

THE NEW BMW 5 SERIES GRAN TURISMO.

BMW EfficientDynamics
Less emissions. More driving pleasure.

Intelligent two-piece tailgate delivers flexible solutions for loading.

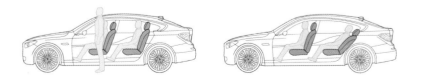

Comfortable first class seating offers more room for thought.

00km). Combined 25.2 – 43.5 mpg (11.2 – 6.5 ltr/100km). CO_2 emissions 263 – 173 g/km. BMW EfficientDynamics reduces BMW emissions without

ever closer. Around the 30 glittering tables, the talk was about the week ahead and of the impending work scheduled for the West Course itself.

Over the past few years, Ernie Els has been heavily involved in the modernisation and refinement of the course set-up and the South African will oversee the final piece of the jigsaw over the next 12 months when all 18 greens will be rebuilt using modern construction to ensure they perform to the absolute highest standards.

This mammoth undertaking, including reseeding of the fairways and green surrounds, will not only maintain the West Course's justified reputation for all-round excellence but will offer an even more impressive stage for the BMW PGA Championship next year. This will be some achievement given the fact the old course has proved a worthy backdrop over many years for the talents of everyone you could possibly imagine should be listed in a Golfing Who's Who.

This big-scale tinkering offers yet another tantalising reason to relish the prospect of the 2010 Championship. It will, however, take something very special to surpass the entertainment on offer in 2009. From Casey's all-round play, to defending champion Miguel Angel Jiménez's albatross two at the fourth hole in the final round and former Open Champion Ben Curtis' birdie-birdie-eagle-eagle finish on Sunday, there was much to delight the 80,186 spectators.

To sum up, "просто сенсационный" as our security guard friend might say. "Simply sensational" will do for the rest of us.

Bill Elliott
The Observer

Søren Kjeldsen

Above Robert Karlsson, winner of The 2008 Harry Vardon Trophy, was presented with the award by eight-time winner Colin Montgomerie at The European Tour's Annual Dinner
Below The Tour Players' Foundation – The European Tour's registered charity – marked its rebranding by presenting a cheque for £35,000 to Children with Special Needs, a local charity to The European Tour's Wentworth HQ. Henrik Stenson (centre) and Mark Roe (second left) presented a cheque to representatives of the CWSN at Wentworth Club

Stephen Dodd

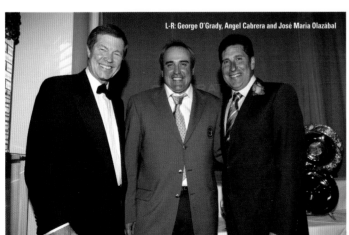

L-R: George O'Grady, Angel Cabrera and José Maria Olazábal

THE EUROPEAN OPEN
The London Golf Club (Heritage Course)
Ash, Kent, England
May 28–31, 2009

1	**CHRISTIAN CÉVAËR**		67	70	70	74	281	-7
2	Gary Orr		71	72	68	71	282	-6
	Alvaro Quiros		71	70	69	72	282	-6
	Steve Webster		69	72	70	71	282	-6
5	Stephen Dodd		75	70	70	68	283	-5
	Jeev Milkha Singh		67	69	71	76	283	-5
	Chris Wood		69	73	68	73	283	-5
8	Ben Curtis		68	73	75	68	284	-4
	Marcus Fraser		69	70	72	73	284	-4
	Søren Hansen		69	75	67	73	284	-4
	José Manuel Lara		70	68	74	72	284	-4

Christian Cévaër and George O'Grady, Chief Executive of The European Tour

Total Prize Fund €2,043,589   **First Prize** €341,220

"When I was in Spain five years ago I dedicated the victory to my father - this is definitely for my wife Fabienne who is my greatest supporter" — Christian Cévaër

Gonzalo Fernandez-Castaño

HOLE 7
Par 3
187 yards
171 metres

Expert Course

If, at the start of the week, you were asked to pick a winner of The European Open, you could probably make a case for most of the field ahead of Christian Cévaër. Not only was one of the shortest hitters on Tour playing on one of the season's longest courses, stomach problems saw the Frenchman come into the week in not the best of health and also with one eye on his heavily pregnant wife Fabienne who was close to giving birth to their second child.

But golf can be a strange game at times and so it turned out deep in the south of England as Cévaër plotted an expert course round the demanding London Golf Club layout, the mastery of his rescue club approaches matched only by his assuredness around the putting surfaces, all of which added up to a winning seven under par total of 281.

Second place was shared by three players; Scotland's Gary Orr, Spain's Alvaro Quiros and Steve Webster of England, all of whom had their chances over the dramatic closing stages but, in the end, no-one from the chasing pack could come up with the goods to deny Cévaër his second Tour success, five years after his first in the 2004 Canarias Open de España.

Gary Orr

DUBAI
WORLD CHAMPIONSHIP
JUMEIRAH GOLF ESTATES

Jeev Milkha Singh

ROLEX

HOLE 16
Par 4
486 yards
444 metres

Martin Kaymer

THE CELTIC MANOR WALES OPEN
The Celtic Manor Resort (Twenty Ten Course)
City of Newport, Wales
June 4–7, 2009

1	**JEPPE HULDAHL**		69	71	68	67	275	-9
2	Niclas Fasth		71	68	71	66	276	-8
3	Ignacio Garrido		68	69	71	69	277	-7
4	Gary Lockerbie		69	70	74	65	278	-6
	Danny Willett		73	66	72	67	278	-6
6	Simon Dyson		74	65	70	70	279	-5
	Oliver Fisher		72	69	71	67	279	-5
	Richard Green		68	71	71	69	279	-5
	Jeev Milkha Singh		69	68	73	69	279	-5
10	Grégory Bourdy		70	70	70	70	280	-4
	Richie Ramsay		68	67	76	69	280	-4
	Paul Waring		71	68	70	71	280	-4
	Chris Wood		72	69	70	69	280	-4
	Fabrizio Zanotti		67	71	72	70	280	-4

Gareth Edwards CBE, Honorary Captain of The Twenty Ten Club and Jeppe Huldahl

Total Prize Fund €2,073,926   **First Prize** €343,086

"I don't know what to say, I didn't even dream of this coming into this week. This is such a big tournament to win, it's unbelievable" – Jeppe Huldahl

Ignacio Garrido

Niclas Fasth

FINE DINING, WELL-BEING, TENNIS, SHOOTING, FOURTEEN HUNDRED ACRES
OF BREATHING SPACE AND THREE STUNNING CHAMPIONSHIP GOLF COURSES.

20 10
the
Twenty
Ten

CELTIC MANOR RESORT

THIS IS THE TWENTY TEN. TAILOR MADE TO CHALLENGE THE BEST.
THIS IS WHERE DRAGONS PLAY
THIS IS THE FIRST COURSE IN HISTORY BUILT TO HOST THE RYDER CUP.

RYDER CUP
1927 2010
CELTIC MANOR

reservations +44 (0) 1633 410262   celtic-manor.com

Changed Days

Almost exactly a year ago to the day, Jeppe Huldahl was competing in Manchester in the Oceânico Group Pro-Am on the European Challenge Tour where he won €1,200 for finishing 28th. Not a huge amount, granted, but nevertheless money which helped him finish tenth on the Rankings at the end of the year to guarantee his European Tour playing privileges for the 2009 season. The value of that was illustrated perfectly when he claimed his maiden victory in The Celtic Manor Wales Open and picked up a cheque for €343,086 in the process in addition to a playing exemption until the end of the 2011 season.

It was a victory richly deserved for the 26 year old Dane who had grabbed control of proceedings at the end of the weather-affected third round, staying patient amidst the delays to post a 68, before easing to a one shot victory over Sweden's Niclas Fasth with a final round 67 for a winning nine under par total of 275.

Fasth battled gamely to make up his two shot overnight deficit in the final round, especially in the eight holes from the sixth to the 13th, a stretch he covered in figures of five under par, but two late dropped shots ended his title quest.

Below L-R: Sir Terry Matthews, Chairman of The Celtic Manor Resort; Rt Hon Rhodri Morgan, First Minister for Wales; and George O'Grady, Chief Executive of The European Tour, addressed the media prior to The 2009 Celtic Manor Wales Open and looked ahead to The 2010 Ryder Cup

Danny Willett

European Ryder Cup Captain Colin Montgomerie (left) and his American counterpart Corey Pavin gave their first joint press conference ahead of The 2010 Ryder Cup at The Celtic Manor Resort

Paul McGinley

"This is a massive win for me and I am so happy. There were a lot of thoughts going through my head so I was extremely pleased at how I handled the pressure" — Christian Nilsson

SAINT-OMER OPEN presented by Neuflize OBC
Aa Saint Omer Golf Club
Lumbres, France
June 18-21, 2009

1	**CHRISTIAN NILSSON**		68	69	65	69	271	-13
2	José-Filipe Lima		69	71	69	68	277	-7
3	Javier Colomo		73	71	71	66	281	-3
	Lorenzo Gagli		71	71	68	71	281	-3
	Richard McEvoy		72	74	68	67	281	-3
	Åke Nilsson		71	71	68	71	281	-3
7	Sion E Bebb		70	72	67	73	282	-2
	James Morrison		67	69	70	76	282	-2
	Andrew Tampion		69	70	73	70	282	-2
10	Stuart Manley		71	71	70	71	283	-1
	Edoardo Molinari		73	71	69	70	283	-1
	Steven O'Hara		72	70	72	69	283	-1
	Inder Van Weerelt		73	73	71	66	283	-1
	Kane Webber		70	71	74	68	283	-1

Christian Nilsson and Jean-Jacques Durand, Championship Director

Total Prize Fund €606,237   **First Prize €100,000**

José-Filipe Lima

Edoardo Molinari

James Morrison

Second Time Around

There is a commonly held belief among golfers that you learn more about yourself through losing a tournament than winning one. The trick, however, is to put that experience to good use the next time you are faced with a chance to succeed; Christian Nilsson showed just how to do that.

Last year the Swede found himself in the ideal position to win the SAINT-OMER OPEN presented by Neuflize OBC having taken command of the tournament at the halfway stage, but had to settle for second as Englishman David Dixon came through to triumph.

Fast forward 12 months and the 30 year old from Karlstad was in the identical place, holding pole position as the tournament moved into its final round but this time Nilsson made no mistake, a bogey free round of 69 turning his four shot advantage at the start of the day into a six shot winning total over second placed José-Filipe Lima, with the rest of the field a distant spot on the horizon.

Nilsson's reward was a European Tour exemption until the end of the 2010 season while Lima moved up to third on the Challenge Tour rankings, such dual rewards available from the only tournament on the 2009 calendar to be part of both schedules.

On Cloud Nine

US OPEN CHAMPIONSHIP
Bethpage State Park (Black Course)
Farmingdale, New York, USA
June 18-21, 2009

1	**LUCAS GLOVER**		69	64	70	73	276	-4
2	Ricky Barnes		67	65	70	76	278	-2
	David Duval		67	70	70	71	278	-2
	Phil Mickelson		69	70	69	70	278	-2
5	Ross Fisher		70	68	69	72	279	-1
6	Søren Hansen		70	71	70	69	280	0
	Hunter Mahan		72	68	68	72	280	0
	Tiger Woods		74	69	68	69	280	0
9	Henrik Stenson		73	70	70	68	281	1
10	Stephen Ames		74	66	70	72	282	2
	Matt Bettencourt		75	67	71	69	282	2
	Sergio Garcia		70	70	72	70	282	2
	Rory McIlroy		72	70	72	68	282	2
	Ryan Moore		70	69	72	71	282	2
	Mike Weir		64	70	74	74	282	2

Jim Vernon, President of the USGA and Lucas Glover

Total Prize Fund €5,288,326   **First Prize** €952,152

"I had a good week of preparation and came here with a good attitude.
It was the best ball striking week I've ever had and I'm obviously very
excited and honoured to have won"

— Lucas Glover

Ten days after his stunning triumph at Bethpage State Park, Lucas Glover announced he was "still up in the clouds." It was a perfectly apt description considering the weather conditions from which he had emerged to claim his first Major Championship title.

Søren Hansen

Huge black clouds had hung over New York State for the majority of the week, carrying a seemingly inexhaustible supply of rain together with equal measures of frustration and uncertainty. In fact, as the 29 year old from South Carolina was presented with the famous old trophy on Monday afternoon, it was difficult to know for whom to have more admiration.

Was it Glover, for surviving this test of stamina and patience, or the greenkeeping staff for managing to ensure a finish before midweek? Their wonderful Black Course had been saturated to the point of being flooded, yet somehow they had managed to keep the 109th US Open Championship afloat.

Monday's drama was the reward for their ceaseless toils. Suddenly, through all the puddles, the interruptions and the ripped-up schedules, an enthralling golf tournament emerged. Glover was to prove the ultimate protagonist, although there were other heroes in this show. Not least England's Ross Fisher who, for a long time in the final round, seemed set to break Europe's void in the tournament stretching all the way back to Tony Jacklin's triumph at Hazeltine National in 1970.

An eagle three at the 13th pulled him to within a shot of Glover but he found the rough with his next drive and the ensuing bogey saw his momentum falter. However, his closing 72 for fifth place, only three shots adrift of the eventual champion, was a laudable performance.

The Englishman was not alone in leaving Long Island believing he had allowed glory to slip through his fingers. Incredibly, Phil Mickelson finished runner-up in a US Open for the fifth time and, with due respect to

Glover, much of the week was about the left-hander.

It was at Bethpage State Park in 2002 where his love affair with the east coast galleries began and seven years later he was back to compete in what was always going to be an emotional occasion. His wife, Amy, was at home in California preparing to begin treatment for breast cancer and without his usual support base, Mickelson reached out to the crowd. Boy, how they responded.

Indeed, as the action entered its decisive hours it was all too easy to forget that this was a work day. Thousands thronged the fairways as Mickelson went on a charge and when he tied Glover for the lead with five holes remaining, the atmosphere duly went with him. However, when he bogeyed the 15th and 17th with missed short putts, groans filled the air, leaving the stage for Glover to command.

Phil Mickelson

Glover played in the final group with Ricky Barnes, the former US Amateur champion who had been the hero of those rain-ravaged opening days when rounds of 67-65 saw him record an eight under par total of 132, a score which entered the record books as the lowest halfway total in US Open history.

Barnes held the lead going into the final round but, as he faltered, Glover overcame an early stumble to show commendable poise as the clubhouse loomed. He bogeyed the 15th but nervelessly birdied the 16th and a 73 for a four under par total of 276 proved good enough for a two shot victory over a resurgent David Duval, Barnes and Mickelson.

"No doubt this was a test of patience," said the man who started the week in 71st place on the Official

Ross Fisher

Go on, the world awaits.

United offers you North America like no other airline, with 11 daily flights from London Heathrow to five gateway cities* Chicago, Denver, Los Angeles, San Francisco and Washington, D.C. United can take you to over 170 U.S. cities.

For more information or to book visit **www.unitedairlines.co.uk**.

⦙⦙UNITED
It's time to fly.®

Sergio Garcia

Henrik Stenson

World Golf Ranking. "It was tough, but the golf course played fantastically well. The birdie at the 16th was massive. I guess if I can win this, I should be able to play all right every week. It will definitely be a big confidence boost."

Glover has always been known to possess talent but it is fair to say, having missed the cut in his three previous US Opens and having only one prior US PGA Tour victory to his name, he did not come into the event as one of the fancied competitors.

In fact, the overwhelming majority of those who punted with heads rather than hearts would have sided with Tiger Woods. However, the World Number One's putter proved to be wasteful and, despite launching a mini-charge on the back nine of the final round, a 15th Major Championship title never looked realistic.

Still, a tie for sixth place with his fellow American Hunter Mahan and Denmark's Søren Hansen, who once again put in another fine performance on the world stage, was pretty remarkable considering his travails on the greens and, if anything, he headed to Turnberry for The Open Championship in confident mood.

While the World Number One began his preparations, the World Number Two revealed he would not be travelling to Scotland. "I've got more important things going on," said Mickelson. It didn't really need saying.

James Corrigan
The Independent

"It is no secret that I haven't played well since 2007 and 2008 was a terrible year for me in more ways than one, so it's great to win again. Today, I was superb" — Nick Dougherty

BMW INTERNATIONAL OPEN
Golfclub München Eichenried
Munich, Germany
June 25-28, 2009

EUROPEAN TOUR
RACE TO
DUBAI
2009

Pos	Player		R1	R2	R3	R4	Total	Par
1	**Nick DOUGHERTY**		69	65	68	64	266	-22
2	Rafa Echenique		68	69	68	62	267	-21
3	Retief Goosen		64	68	67	71	270	-18
4	Felipe Aguilar		69	70	66	66	271	-17
	David Drysdale		70	64	68	69	271	-17
	Miguel Angel Jiménez		69	67	70	65	271	-17
	Graeme Storm		70	70	64	67	271	-17
8	Shiv Kapur		71	66	70	65	272	-16
9	Richard Green		71	68	68	66	273	-15
	James Kingston		67	69	67	70	273	-15
	Søren Kjeldsen		68	65	70	70	273	-15
	Bernhard Langer		68	68	65	72	273	-15
	Thomas Levet		68	67	70	68	273	-15
	Danny Willett		67	68	71	67	273	-15

Nick Dougherty and Dr. Friedrich Eichiner, Member of the Board, BMW Group

Total Prize Fund €2,003,000   **First Prize** €333,330

Bernhard Langer

Graeme Storm

Rafa Echenique

93

LET UPS LOOK AFTER YOUR LONG GAME...

SO YOU CAN FOCUS ON YOUR SHORT GAME.

In business, as in golf, winning means getting things of importance where they need to be, quickly and accurately. That's why the European Tour chooses a logistics partner that can reliably deliver. All the way from the tee to the pin.

www.ups.com/europeantour

Deliver more

Retief Goosen

Felipe Aguilar

Back on Track

Every golfer, at the moment of triumph, experiences a surge of emotion but for some, that feeling is made more intense for reasons outside golf – Nick Dougherty knows all about that.

When the Englishman rolled in his par putt on the final green for victory in the BMW International Open, he immediately raised his eyes and pointed his finger to the heavens, a touching gesture in honour of his beloved mother Ennis who had passed away the previous spring.

Having had such an influence on his life and his golf, it was little surprise that Dougherty's game suffered in the aftermath but the 27 year old's performance in Germany proved he was firmly back on track.

Going into the final round in third place, adrift of Major Champions Retief Goosen and Bernhard Langer, Dougherty conjured up a sensational Sunday, birdieing the first three holes, and nine altogether, for a 64 and a winning 22 under par total of 266. He finished one clear of Rafa Echenique who produced one of the most remarkable finishes in European Tour history.

The Argentine holed his three iron second shot from 243 yards for the first albatross on the 18th in the tournament's 21 years. It helped him to a 62 for 267 and was a shot later voted European Tour Shot of the Month for June.

"This is a very special moment for me. I've had some good chances to win on Tour since Germany last year but didn't take them, so this is great" – Martin Kaymer

ALSTOM

OPEN DE FRANCE ALSTOM
Le Golf National (Albatross Course)
Paris, France
June 2-5, 2009

1	**MARTIN KAYMER**		62	72	69	68	271	-13
2	Lee Westwood		68	68	70	65	271	-13
3	Ian Poulter		72	69	66	67	274	-10
4	Anders Hansen		69	72	68	66	275	-9
	Peter Hanson		65	70	70	70	275	-9
6	Kenneth Ferrie		70	68	71	67	276	-8
	Richard Green		68	67	70	71	276	-8
	Søren Hansen		68	71	72	65	276	-8
	Paul Waring		66	70	68	72	276	-8
10	Gareth Maybin		69	71	71	67	278	-6
	Scott Strange		65	72	71	70	278	-6
	Danny Willett		68	71	70	69	278	-6

Patrick Kron, Chairman and C.E.O., ALSTOM, and Martin Kaymer

Total Prize Fund €4,047,916   **First Prize** €666,660

Lee Westwood

Ian Poulter

Paul Waring

Peter Hanson

End to End

If anyone needed an illustration of how to perfectly bookend a golf tournament, then Martin Kaymer provided it on his way to victory in the Open de France ALSTOM.

The 24 year old German began the week in scintillating fashion, equalling the course record with a nine under par 62, and ended it equally as impressively, needing only one hole of a sudden-death play-off to see off the challenge of England's Lee Westwood.

Kaymer, whose second European Tour success had come just over a year ago in the BMW International Open in Munich, slipped out of pole position after

his first round heroics but did enough to book a spot in the final group on the last day alongside Rafa Echenique.

As the Argentine slipped back, Westwood set the clubhouse target with a fine 65 for 13 under par total of 271, an aggregate subsequently matched by Kaymer's 68. On their return to the 18th hole moments later, the Englishman's good fortune ran out as his approach shot found the water hazard from where he pitched out but missed his putt for bogey five. It left Kaymer, on the green in three, with two putts for the title but he finished with a flourish, requiring only one.

Miguel Angel Jiménez receives
an engraved ice bucket from Tournament Director
David Probyn to commemorate his 500th European Tour appearance

BARCLAYS
SCOTTISH OPEN

THE BARCLAYS SCOTTISH OPEN
Loch Lomond Golf Club
Glasgow, Scotland
July 9–12, 2009

1	**MARTIN KAYMER**		69	65	66	69	269	-15
2	Gonzalo Fernandez-Castaño		65	70	64	72	271	-13
	Raphaël Jacquelin		67	72	66	66	271	-13
4	Søren Kjeldsen		67	68	67	70	272	-12
	Adam Scott		66	67	73	66	272	-12
6	Retief Goosen		68	63	69	73	273	-11
	Nick Watney		67	68	71	67	273	-11
8	Ross Fisher		69	67	71	67	274	-10
	Lee Westwood		73	66	64	71	274	-10
10	Martin Laird		65	70	69	71	275	-9

Martin Kaymer and Robert E Diamond Jr, President, Barclays PLC

Total Prize Fund €3,512,475   **First Prize** €579,339

"If you win in Scotland, the home of golf, it is always extra special. I really enjoyed the week here and the way that the fans got behind me – they were amazing" – Martin Kaymer

Adam Scott

Raphaël Jacquelin

Gonzalo Fernandez-Castaño

Søren Kjeldsen

UNWAVERING FOCUS
WHEN THE PRESSURE'S ON.

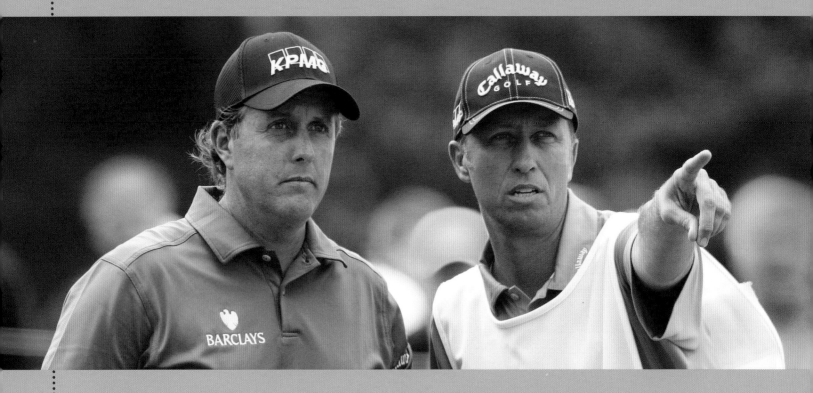

By focusing on our clients we provide strategic advisory, financing
and risk management solutions for all market conditions.

Earn Success Every Day

BARCLAYS CAPITAL

Ernie Els

Two Good

Conventional wisdom states that the week after you win a tournament on The European Tour International Schedule, you are so drained, both mentally and physically, that you cannot be expected to perform to any standard the following week. If that is the case, then no-one shared that particular script with Martin Kaymer.

Seven days after beating Lee Westwood in a play-off to claim the Open de France ALSTOM, the German was on the title trail once again, four sublime rounds in the 60s good enough for a two shot victory over Spain's Gonzalo Fernandez-Castaño and Raphaël Jacquelin of France in

The Barclays Scottish Open. It was a performance which moved Kaymer to second place in The Race to Dubai and to 11th on the Official World Golf Ranking and one which also saw his earnings for the two week period reach an eye popping total of €1,246,000.

Australian Richard Green, South African Retief Goosen – the course record holder and winner of the event in 2001 – and Fernandez-Castaño had the honour of leading the way at the end of rounds one, two and three respectively, but when it came to the crunch no-one could top Kaymer who followed Richard Sterne as a back-to-back winner in the 2009 season.

THE OPEN CHAMPIONSHIP

THE 138TH OPEN CHAMPIONSHIP
Ailsa Course, Turnberry
Ayrshire, Scotland
July 16-19, 2009

Stewart Cink and Peter Wiseman, Captain of Turnberry Golf Club

Pos	Player		R1	R2	R3	R4	Total	Par
1	**STEWART CINK**		66	72	71	69	278	-2
2	Tom Watson		65	70	71	72	278	-2
3	Lee Westwood		68	70	70	71	279	-1
	Chris Wood		70	70	72	67	279	-1
5	Luke Donald		71	72	70	67	280	0
	Mathew Goggin		66	72	69	73	280	0
	Retief Goosen		67	70	71	72	280	0
8	Thomas Aiken		71	72	69	69	281	1
	Ernie Els		69	72	72	68	281	1
	Søren Hansen		68	72	74	67	281	1
	Richard S Johnson		70	72	69	70	281	1
	Justin Leonard		70	70	73	68	281	1

Total Prize Fund €4,857,633   **First Prize** €866,557

Grace and Dignity

HOLE	PAR	PLAYER		SCORE	CUML.		PLAYER		SCORE FOR RND
70	-2	WATSON T.	*		AFTER **71** HOLES				
70	-1	WESTWOOD					GAME 35		
69	-1	GOGGIN					FURYK		
72	-1	WOOD C.		279	+5		GOOSEN		
71	-1	CINK			E		GAME 34		
72	E	DONALD		280	+7		MOLDER		
71	E	GOOSEN			-1		CINK		

Turnberry 2009

www.opengolf.com

"I am just filled with pride and honour. There are too many words to use right now to describe how I am feeling – but it can't get any more satisfying than this" — Stewart Cink

Some weeks before The Open Championship I had the pleasure of interviewing Thomas Sturges Watson. Chatting with stars is not always a delight but with Watson it most certainly is.

He talked a lot about his life, both as a golfer and as a man, and happily relived those thrilling days at Turnberry in 1977 when he went head to head with Jack Nicklaus and triumphed in the quest for the Claret Jug; the ruggedly sensational stretch of Ayrshire coast illuminated by a relentless sun while, at the same time, being backlit by the brilliance of two players in their prime.

When asked why he still bothered to try and compete at the highest level, why the old game still had him in its most intimate grasp, his answer was simple. "Because golf is in my soul and because I still have a real passion for it," he said. As Turnberry 2009 unfolded before our startled and delighted gaze, his straightforward reply resonated even more.

Eventually, for the record books, Stewart Cink's triumph will be the only fact that matters. This, however, is for some future generation. For now, The 138th Open Championship will be recalled as the one that Watson, a few weeks short of his 60th birthday could, and should, have won.

This fact is not to deny the younger American his own moment in the sun, it is simply to emphasise the wonder of Watson's challenge. In the end, only his old putting demons denied him the most unlikely and gloriously improbable victory in sporting history.

After four days of attention-grabbing golf, of incident and delight, it all came down to an eight foot putt on the final green. Hole it and Watson would have a win to celebrate through all the ages, miss it and he would be in a play-off. Of course, he missed. Not only missed but struck one of the worst putts of his career just when he needed one of his best.

At that moment, as his ball slid both short and right of the hole, the packed stands let out a collective sigh of disappointment. At the same moment, Watson slumped forward, his shoulders caved and the

energy he had offered a delighted audience all week, began to seep from his pores.

It was as though he had just woken up from a dream to face, fleetingly, a living nightmare. Before The Open began, he had spoken about locating a feeling of spirituality as he practised on the ancient links. To some, this psychology graduate from Harvard was turning too maudlin too soon. As it turned out, he wasn't.

He admitted he felt, as he played, the presence of his long-time caddie and friend Bruce Edwards, who was taken too early by ALS (Lou Gehrig's Disease) at the age of 49 in 2004. No matter how the more secular among us may view this sort of thing, there was no doubting that Tom Watson was a man inspired.

So, too, were others. Nicklaus, still struggling to get to grips with the art of

Chris Wood

Lee Westwood

Tom Watson

Retief Goosen

Luke Donald

Ross Fisher

texting on a mobile phone, got his wife Barbara to send his old adversary a message on Sunday morning. It read: 'Do it for the old guys. Make us cry again.' That Watson failed to follow the first command but managed to succeed with the latter is now a matter of forlorn fact. Yet, if ever there was some sort victory in defeat, then he found it.

Cink, meanwhile, found more than just his first Major Championship win. The brilliance of his final round 69 was exceeded only by the exquisiteness of his golf during a four hole play-off that swiftly turned into a procession. This, in turn, was usurped by his grace and dignity in his greatest moment of triumph.

Cink knew what he was doing and knew he had to do it too. He realised that he was the unwanted intruder, the destroyer of the dream. His was a nasty job but it had to be done and he did it with outstanding golf, wit and sensitivity. This will not make its way into too many history books but it will be what many of us will remember when we reflect on these four days in Ayrshire.

We will also recall that Tiger Woods, out of sorts and out of the Championship at the halfway stage for the first time ever, was as surprising a golfer this week as Watson was a revelation. We will also recount, too, that Lee Westwood will, perhaps, never have a better chance and that only his last hole lapse cost him a spot in the play-off.

Always, however, we will return to Watson. Henry Thoreau, the great 19th Century American thinker, once said: "None are so old as those who have outlived enthusiasm."

Judged by Thoreau's thought, Tom Watson is still taking his first steps. But then, he did have a new hip installed only eight months before he travelled to Scotland. An extraordinary man as well as a great, great golfer.

Bill Elliott
The Observer

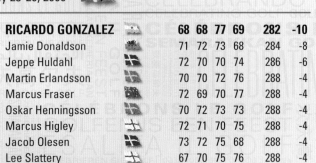

SAS Masters

SAS MASTERS
Barsebäck Golf and Country Club
Malmö, Sweden
July 23-26, 2009

#								
1	**RICARDO GONZALEZ**		**68**	**68**	**77**	**69**	**282**	**-10**
2	Jamie Donaldson		71	72	73	68	284	-8
3	Jeppe Huldahl		72	70	70	74	286	-6
4	Martin Erlandsson		70	70	72	76	288	-4
	Marcus Fraser		72	69	70	77	288	-4
	Oskar Henningsson		70	72	73	73	288	-4
	Marcus Higley		72	71	70	75	288	-4
	Jacob Olesen		73	72	75	68	288	-4
	Lee Slattery		67	70	75	76	288	-4
	Nathan Smith		75	71	71	71	288	-4

Lars Philipsson, Vice President SAS and Ricardo Gonzalez

Total Prize Fund €1,011,916   **First Prize** €166,660

"It's been a hard year but I was always fighting, fighting, fighting. You can always make it if you work hard and never lose faith and I think I've proved that" – Ricardo Gonzalez

Jamie Donaldson

Lee Slattery

Jeppe Huldahl

The Axeman

Argentine golfers love a nickname. Angel Cabrera is affectionately known as 'El Pato' – The Duck, while Eduardo Romero goes by the soubriquet 'El Gato' – The Cat. Now there is another one to add to the list, Ricardo Gonzalez is now 'El Hombre del Hacha', or The Axeman.

The moniker materialised after the 40 year old from Corrientes failed to qualify for the previous week's Open Championship at Turnberry and returned home to take out his frustrations – by chopping down trees on his farm.

The unusual therapy certainly paid dividends as Gonzalez returned to action a new man and proved it in style by winning his fourth European Tour title in the SAS Masters, a ten under par total of 282 sufficient for a two shot triumph over Welshman Jamie Donaldson.

It was a remarkable turnaround in fortunes for one of the Tour's longest hitters, who still packed plenty of power but who had lacked accuracy thus far in 2009, not recording a single top ten in his 14 previous outings to languish 153rd in The Race to Dubai.

But all that was put right in Sweden where he successfully combated the momentary blip of a third round 77, three other rounds in the 60s good enough for victory.

"My father Rolf has always been by my side since I started playing golf and it was great he was here this week to see me win. I dedicate this victory to him" — Oskar Henningsson

Moravia Silesia 2009 Open

MORAVIA SILESIA OPEN PRESENTED BY ALO DIAMONDS
Prosper Golf Resort (Old Course)
Čeladná, Czech Republic
July 30-August 3, 2009

1	**OSKAR HENNINGSSON**		70	71	67	67	275	-13
2	Sam Little		70	67	70	70	277	-11
	Steve Webster		66	70	69	72	277	-11
4	Marc Cayeux		71	71	70	66	278	-10
	Ignacio Garrido		67	70	69	72	278	-10
	Graeme Storm		68	68	70	72	278	-10
7	José Manuel Lara		68	70	73	68	279	-9
	Gareth Maybin		73	66	68	72	279	-9
9	Robert-Jan Derksen		67	70	71	72	280	-8
	Tano Goya		65	75	70	70	280	-8

Jaroslav Palas, Governor of Moravia Silesia region and Oskar Henningsson

Total Prize Fund €2,003,000   **First Prize** €333,330

Steve Webster

Sam Little

Graeme Storm

Numbers Game

Golf, by its very essence, is a game of numbers, but the only one Oskar Henningsson was interested in at the conclusion of the Moravia Silesia Open presented by ALO Diamonds was the number one, which perfectly illustrated his first victory on The European Tour International Schedule.

Not that number one is an unusual position for the 23 year old Swede to find himself for he occupied the self same spot in the 2008 Qualifying School Final Stage in Spain.

In triumphing in the Czech Republic however, Henningsson added his own numbers to golf's record books;

becoming not only the 31st player to graduate from the Qualifying School and post a win the following season, but also only the third player behind Gordon Brand Jnr and José Maria Olazábal to triumph the season after winning the Final Stage itself.

Going into the final round in a share of sixth spot, three shots adrift of leader Steve Webster, Henningsson knew he had to make a fast start and did just that when he reached the turn in 32. With Webster slipping back and no other contender emerging from the pack, further birdies at the 13th and 16th gave him the cushion which allowed him to bogey the last and still win comfortably.

Ignacio Garrido

"That was a lot of fun and a great battle out there and I know we will definitely do it again in the future. Paddy is a guy I admire very much" — Tiger Woods

WGC - BRIDGESTONE INVITATIONAL

Firestone Country Club (South Course)
Akron, Ohio, USA
August 6-9, 2009

1	**TIGER WOODS**		**68**	**70**	**65**	**65**	**268**	**-12**
2	Robert Allenby		68	69	69	66	272	-8
	Padraig Harrington		64	69	67	72	272	-8
4	Angel Cabrera		70	68	68	67	273	-7
	Hunter Mahan		68	69	70	66	273	-7
6	Stewart Cink		69	69	68	68	274	-6
	Miguel Angel Jiménez		68	72	66	68	274	-6
	Steve Stricker		67	69	71	67	274	-6
9	Lee Westwood		69	71	70	65	275	-5
10	Mike Weir		71	66	69	70	276	-4

Richard Hills, European Ryder Cup Director and Tiger Woods

Total Prize Fund €6,017,682   **First Prize** €999,407

Angel Cabrera

Robert Allenby

Breathtaking Battle

Did you hear the one about the Irishman and the American? It sounds like the start of some bad joke but for the world of golf it is deadly serious and could well be the central theme of the game's top events for years to come.

Three-time Major Champion Padraig Harrington and World Number One Tiger Woods are, without doubt, two of the top players in the game at the present time and proved that conclusively with a breathtaking battle in the WGC – Bridgestone Invitational.

The Irishman lit the blue touchpaper with an opening 64, a round which propelled him into the lead and into a position he maintained through Friday

and Saturday. Going into the final round, he held a three shot lead over playing partner Woods but that quickly evaporated in the face of a blistering start by the American which saw him move two ahead by the turn.

Grittily, Harrington battled on and his own birdie at the 11th combined with Woods' bogey at the 13th saw the contest level once again. It stayed that way until the pivotal moment on the 16th, Woods firing a sensational eight iron approach to a foot for a birdie four, while Harrington found the water on his way to a triple bogey eight. It was game over this time – here's to the next showdown.

Oliver Wilson

Impervious and Impressive

"You never know in life, this might be my last win as a golfer but if it is, it sure is a great day. It hasn't really sunk in yet, but I know the significance of what I've done"

— Y E Yang

US PGA CHAMPIONSHIP
Hazeltine National Golf Club
Chaska, Minnesota, USA
August 13-16, 2009

1	**Y E YANG**		**73**	**70**	**67**	**70**	**280**	**-8**
2	Tiger Woods		67	70	71	75	283	-5
3	Rory McIlroy		71	73	71	70	285	-3
	Lee Westwood		70	72	73	70	285	-3
5	Lucas Glover		71	70	71	74	286	-2
6	Ernie Els		75	68	70	74	287	-1
	Martin Kaymer		73	70	71	73	287	-1
	Søren Kjeldsen		70	73	70	74	287	-1
	Henrik Stenson		73	71	68	75	287	-1
10	Padraig Harrington		68	73	69	78	288	0
	Dustin Johnson		72	73	73	70	288	0
	Zach Johnson		74	73	70	71	288	0
	Graeme McDowell		70	75	71	72	288	0
	John Merrick		72	72	74	70	288	0
	Francesco Molinari		74	73	69	72	288	0

Jim Remy, President of the PGA of America and Y E Yang

Total Prize Fund €5,223,214   **First Prize** €942,125

Had the Philistines written the bible, David might have been acknowledged as a decent exponent of the slingshot ... yet the real thrust of their story would have been the 'end of an era' for their own favourite, Goliath. So it was for Y E Yang after felling golf's own Goliath, Tiger Woods, in an unforgettable final round at the US PGA Championship.

Naturally, the 37 year old was feted as the first Asian to win one of golf's four Major Championships. Yet the metamorphosis of this son of a South Korean farming family into a Tiger slayer was neither explored nor explained with as much vim and vigour as the final day demise of Woods.

Which is a pity, as Yang's exceptional effort on Sunday afternoon at Hazeltine National Golf Club was an object lesson to every golfer on the planet on how to achieve the 'seemingly' impossible. Up to that point, 14 times without fail, Woods had taken the lead into the final round of a Major and won.

So an air of inevitability hung over the rural Minnesota town of Chaska that day with the belief that, if there was any threat to the World Number One, it appeared likely to come from defending champion Padraig Harrington. Apparently, no-one showed Yang this particular script.

Playing with Woods for the first time is said to be intimidating but doing it in the final group on Sunday in a Major increases the daunting factor exponentially. Yang, however, seemed wonderfully impervious to it all as he carded a two under par 70, five better than Woods, to win by three.

The key points were well-chronicled – Yang's telling par save from sand at the 13th; his mesmeric 25 yard chip for eagle two at the short par four 14th and, the pièce de résistance, his imperious 205 yard approach to six feet for birdie at the last.

Of course, the outcome might have been different had Woods tucked away two birdie chances on the opening holes; or had he not three-putted for bogey at the fourth, though one suspects it would have made little impact on an opponent utterly committed to playing his own game, come hell or high water.

Lee Westwood

Yang's resolve was uncanny for a man playing on Sunday at a Major for only the third time, even if it would go largely unobserved until the denouement, as international attention turned to the many other factors which emerged from a memorable championship.

One of the main talking points was a weekend of spectacular success for European golf with, in total, eight European born players – Martin Kaymer, Søren Kjeldsen, Graeme McDowell, Rory McIlroy, Francesco Molinari, Henrik Stenson, Lee Westwood and Harrington – finishing in the top 15, with tournament rookie McIlroy and Westwood most prominent in a tie for third.

Following on from that, it is worth noting that, of the 12 players who made the cut in all four Majors in 2009, the leading five against par were: Ross Fisher (+2), McDowell and Stenson (+3), Westwood (+4) and McIlroy (+5). Given Harrington's recent feats, too, Europe has truly arrived at the dawn of a new golden era at golf's top table.

Francesco Molinari

Henrik Stenson

Graeme McDowell

LESS IS MORE.

It's time to work smarter. With less budget, less staff and less time to show an ROI, the paradox is making less offer more. Businesses and governments need to transform the way they do business—for new efficiencies in cost, reliability and performance with less complexity. Cycles of change create unprecedented competitive opportunities for organizations visionary enough to optimize their spend vs. trying to cut their way to success. The challenge is how to do more with less.

Unisys helps clients make less do more by securing their operations, increasing the efficiencies in their data centers, enhancing user productivity and collaboration, and modernizing their business-critical applications.

Refresh your perspective. Let us show you how less can be more.

UNISYS
imagine it. done.

Rory McIlroy

Søren Kjeldsen

compulsory military service, one year of it spent standing guard outside a naval base.

Though his devotion to his sport was unwavering, Yang retained a gregarious, outgoing personality and he is warmly embraced on Tour. "He's very much one of the guys," explained Harrington. "Some of the Asian players travel with a big entourage but Y E is generally there on his own, mixes well, and the guys find him very entertaining."

He is accomplished as a golfer, too, as he proved by beating a world class field, including Woods, in the 2007 HSBC Champions, calming any nerves he felt about playing with Retief Goosen in the final group on Sunday in precisely the same way that he would go on to do at Hazeltine.

Yang admitted he had been nervous on Sunday morning in Minnesota. "I had a rough night but as soon as I got onto the first tee, I became myself," he said: "I did that because it was what I'd always dreamed about. I'd always envisioned myself playing Tiger on the final day at a Major.

"It's not like you're fighting Tiger and he's going to bite you or swing at you with his nine iron. The worst you can do is just lose and go down a few places on the scoreboard. The odds were against me so I really had nothing much at stake and that's how I played it."

Yang was blessed with an irresistible mix of humility and self-confidence that Sunday. He looked Woods in the eye, acknowledged his greatness, but trusted himself and his game enough to simply go out and play. And it worked.

Karl MacGinty
Irish Independent

While all this was going on, golf fans rubber-necked as Woods spun out of control on the final lap of a race he had dominated since the previous Thursday. Was it just a fender-bender or was he feeling the weight of history as he neared the record 18 Major titles won by Jack Nicklaus?

Geopolitically though, how apt it was for golf to celebrate its first Asian Major winner in the week of its first step back on the road of acceptance into the Olympic family?

So much went on at Hazeltine, we glossed over the real story. Yang only found golf at 19 when he ripped apart his anterior cruciate knee ligament while weightlifting. It shattered his dreams of a career in the iron-pumping industry but perhaps helped explain his 'clean and jerk' celebration over his head with his golf bag on the 18th green.

He caught the golf bug hitting balls with a baseball grip into a net on his native Jeju Island, gleaning basic knowledge from instructional videos. His fascination for the game would then survive 24 months of

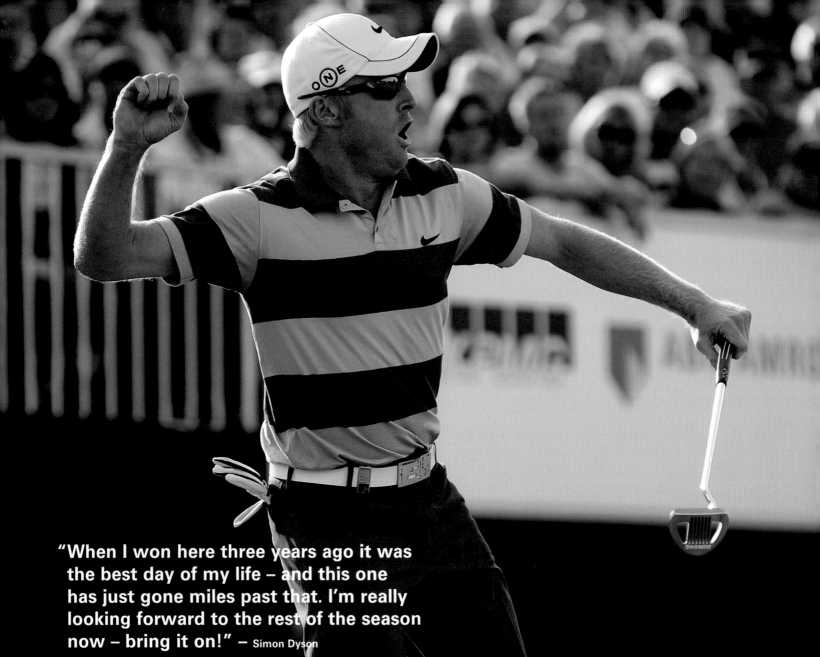

"When I won here three years ago it was the best day of my life – and this one has just gone miles past that. I'm really looking forward to the rest of the season now – bring it on!" – Simon Dyson

KLM OPEN
Kennemer Golf and Country Club
Zandvoort, The Netherlands
August 20-23, 2009

1	**SIMON DYSON**		67	67	68	63	**265**	**-15**
2	Peter Hedblom		66	66	64	69	265	-15
	Peter Lawrie		65	68	65	67	265	-15
4	Damien McGrane		67	67	68	64	266	-14
5	Darren Clarke		65	67	67	68	267	-13
	Jamie Donaldson		66	68	66	67	267	-13
7	Bradley Dredge		66	67	69	66	268	-12
8	Terry Pilkadaris		69	65	66	69	269	-11
9	Niclas Fasth		69	68	67	66	270	-10
10	Ignacio Garrido		66	69	69	67	271	-9
	Alexander Noren		72	66	64	69	271	-9

Simon Dyson and Peter Hartman, CEO KLM

Total Prize Fund €1,793,300   **First Prize** €300,000

Peter Lawrie

Darren Clarke

Peter Hedblom

Bradley Dredge

Simple for Simon

Lightning, it is said, is not supposed to strike twice – try telling that to Simon Dyson after the Englishman captured the KLM Open in extraordinary fashion for the second time in four years.

Just as he did on the same Kennemer course in 2006, the 32 year old sank an 18 foot birdie putt on the first hole of a sudden-death play-off to take the spoils. Three years ago, the stroke ended the hopes of Australian Richard Green, while this time it brought the curtain down on the respective title claims of Ireland's Peter Lawrie and Peter Hedblom of Sweden who had matched Dyson's 15 under par total of 265.

Dyson had been six strokes behind third round leader Hedblom with a round to play but equalled the course record with a closing seven under par 63 to set the mark before producing his final birdie of the day on the first extra hole.

After a recent holiday in Spain, Dyson vowed to knuckle down, giving up caffeine amongst other things and sticking to drinking only water and orange juice for the rest of the season. He admitted it had played a part in this success although he pleaded forgiveness for indulging in a couple of beers to celebrate. We can allow him that.

JOHNNIE WALKER CHAMPIONSHIP AT GLENEAGLES
The Gleneagles Hotel (PGA Centenary Course)
Perthshire, Scotland
August 27–30, 2009

1	**PETER HEDBLOM**		**72**	**68**	**68**	**67**	**275**	**-13**
2	Martin Erlandsson		74	70	70	62	276	-12
3	Grégory Havret		68	76	67	67	278	-10
	Paul Lawrie		67	69	73	69	278	-10
5	Gary Orr		73	71	71	64	279	-9
6	Grégory Bourdy		70	69	71	70	280	-8
	Jamie Donaldson		69	71	70	70	280	-8
	Shiv Kapur		69	70	72	69	280	-8
	Steven O'Hara		68	76	66	70	280	-8
10	Søren Hansen		69	70	71	72	282	-6
	Raphaël Jacquelin		72	69	71	70	282	-6
	Danny Lee		71	70	72	69	282	-6
	David Lynn		76	68	71	67	282	-6

Peter Lederer, Chairman of The Gleneagles Hotel and Peter Hedblom

Total Prize Fund €1,603,154   **First Prize** €269,895

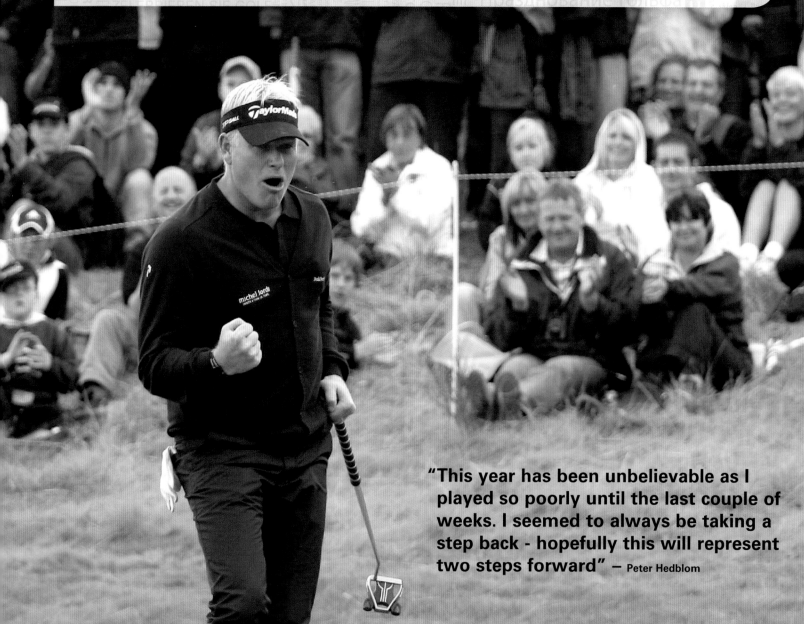

"This year has been unbelievable as I played so poorly until the last couple of weeks. I seemed to always be taking a step back - hopefully this will represent two steps forward" — Peter Hedblom

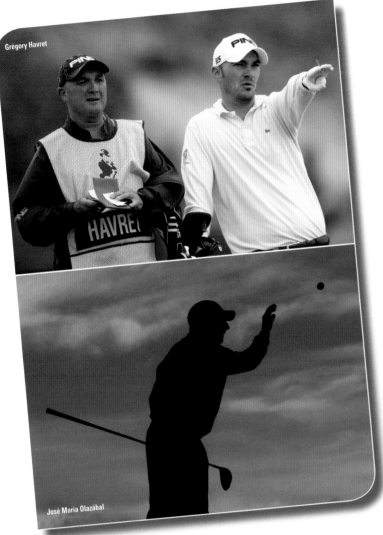

Grégory Havret

HAVRET

José Maria Olazábal

Paul Lawrie

Martin Erlandsson

JOHNNIE WALKER
CHAMPIONSHIP
GLENEAGLES
18
533 YDS 487 m PAR 5

JOHNNIE WALKER®

The PGA Centenary Course, Gleneagles
The host venue for The Ryder Cup in 2014

Scotland
The Perfect Stage

In 2010, Scotland 'The Home of Golf' continues to play host to some of the most high profile events on the European Tour calendar including; the Barclays Scottish Open, Johnnie Walker Championship, Dunhill Links Championship and of course, the return of The Open Championship to the world-famous and iconic St Andrews.

Our continuing relationship with the European Tour, as well as the Challenge and Senior Tours, forms part of our ongoing support of golf in Scotland, as we continue building towards hosting The Ryder Cup in 2014.

To find out more about the work of EventScotland, the national events agency, and why Scotland is the perfect stage for events, please visit our website **EventScotland.org**.

EventScotland

Grégory Bourdy

Shiv Kapur

BBC Radio Five Live hosted an 'At Home With Monty'
discussion forum during the week, live from the European Ryder Cup Captain's
Gleneagles house. Pictured above are the panel, L-R: Derek Lawrenson (Daily Mail Golf Correspondent), Colin
Montgomerie, George O'Grady (European Tour Chief Executive) and Iain Carter (BBC Radio Five Live Golf Correspondent)

Back in the Saddle

They say, if you fall off a horse, the best way to conquer your pain is to get right back in the saddle and Peter Hedblom certainly gave credence to that analogy in golfing terms with his victory in the Johnnie Walker Championship at Gleneagles.

Seven days previously, the 39 year old Swede stood on the verge of his third European Tour title in the KLM Open but was pipped at the post in a sudden-death play-off by England's Simon Dyson.

Just as had been the case in The Netherlands, Hedblom entered the final round in Scotland in the lead but this time kept his nerve on the home straight to breast the finishing

tape with a closing 67 for a 13 under par aggregate of 275 and a one shot victory.

Incredibly, the man who pushed him closest, fellow Swede Martin Erlandsson, began the day in a share of 20th place and not remotely in the radar of potential winners. But he soon put that right with a stunning final round 62, a score which would have set a new record on the PGA Centenary Course but for the preferred lies in operation.

Included in the round was a run of seven successive birdies from the sixth, only one short of the all-time Tour record. Ironically, it proved to be the one shot he needed to force a play-off.

Ω OMEGA

OMEGA EUROPEAN MASTERS
Crans-sur-Sierre
Crans Montana, Switzerland
September 3-6, 2009

1	**ALEX NOREN**		65	70	63	66	264	-20
2	Bradley Dredge		68	65	68	65	266	-18
3	Ross McGowan		67	67	68	65	267	-17
4	Miguel Angel Jiménez		65	68	69	67	269	-15
5	Thongchai Jaidee		65	71	67	67	270	-14
6	Charl Schwartzel		67	68	65	71	271	-13
7	Simon Dyson		63	71	73	65	272	-12
	David Howell		68	69	68	67	272	-12
	Rory McIlroy		67	71	70	64	272	-12
	Angelo Que		69	65	68	70	272	-12

L-R: Stephen Urquhart, President Omega, Alex Noren and Buzz Aldrin, Omega Ambassador

Total Prize Fund €1,996,350   **First Prize** €333,330

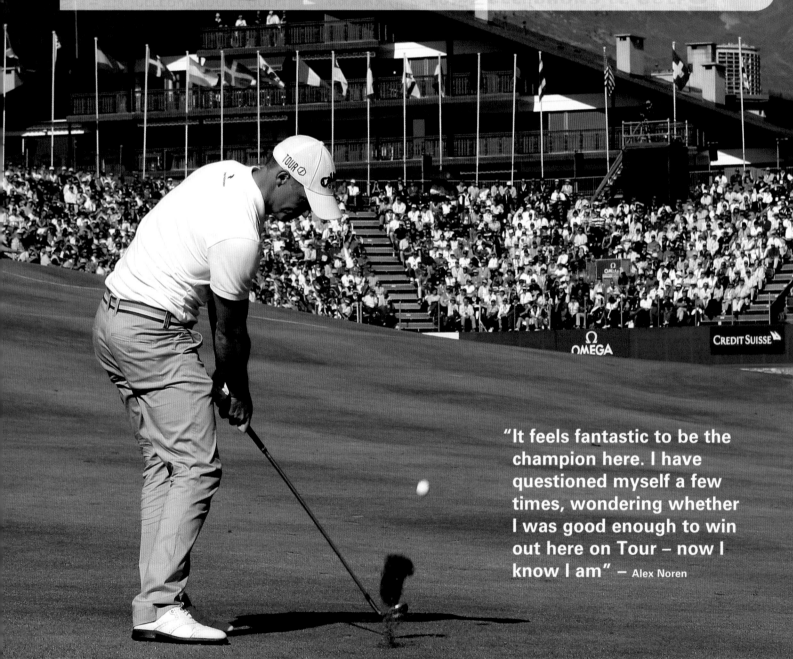

"It feels fantastic to be the champion here. I have questioned myself a few times, wondering whether I was good enough to win out here on Tour – now I know I am" — Alex Noren

Thongchai Jaidee

Bradley Dredge

Ross McGowan

David Howell

The Eagle has Landed

Every champion on The European Tour appreciates there is a crucial moment in the final round when they feel the title is destined to be theirs – for Alex Noren, there was no doubt when that moment arrived.

Up against a charging Bradley Dredge, who was looking to repeat his 2006 Omega European Masters victory, Noren – who led going into the final round – found himself facing a tricky bunker shot at the 15th. But the 27 year old Swede made light of the difficulty of the stroke, flighting the ball beautifully from the sand into the hole for an eagle three.

The shot gave credence to the mantra of his caddie – the experienced Colin Byrne who for

several seasons was on Retief Goosen's bag including during his US Open Championship victory in 2004 – who constantly whispered in Noren's ear in practice the words, 'short game, short game.'

The eagle gave Noren a vital cushion from where he went on to complete his maiden Tour victory, a two shot success in the end over Dredge with Englishman Ross McGowan taking third and Spain's Miguel Angel Jiménez fourth. It also finally convinced the Swede he was free of the injury woes which had blighted his early season, allowing him to live up to the reputation as one of the Scandinavian country's rising stars.

Miguel Angel Jiménez

"My first win on The European Tour in South Africa was important. But I always dreamed about winning my second one somewhere in Europe and I'm delighted to have done that" — James Kingston

 Mercedes-Benz

MERCEDES-BENZ CHAMPIONSHIP
Golf Club Gut Lärchenhof
Cologne, Germany
September 10-13, 2009

1	**JAMES KINGSTON**		67	69	70	69	275	-13
2	Anders Hansen		70	68	70	67	275	-13
3	Simon Dyson		68	70	68	70	276	-12
	Søren Hansen		65	71	70	70	276	-12
	Peter Hanson		70	68	67	71	276	-12
6	Henrik Stenson		70	68	69	71	278	-10
	Anthony Wall		69	70	68	71	278	-10
8	David Drysdale		67	70	73	69	279	-9
	Lee Westwood		70	69	72	68	279	-9
10	Alex Cejka		70	72	68	70	280	-8
	Rodney Pampling		71	72	69	68	280	-8

L-R: Anders Sundt Jensen, Head of Marketing Communications, Mercedes-Benz Car Group, James Kingston and Bernhard Langer

Total Prize Fund €2,000,000   **First Prize** €320,000

Lee Westwood

Changing Fortunes

For most professional golfers, precise preparation is the key to tournament success – but perhaps James Kingston has shown there are other ways. His victory in Cologne was his second European Tour triumph and, incredibly, both wins came in events he did not believe he was even playing.

After an injury blighted spell in the lead-up to the 2008 South African Airways Open the 39 year old felt he would not be able to compete, yet opted to give it a go at the last minute. The result? A one shot victory.

Fast forward 18 months and Kingston believed he was not in the field for the Mercedes-Benz Championship until a

late entry came his way by virtue of his 2008 ranking. The result? A sudden-death play-off victory at the first extra hole over Denmark's Anders Hansen after both men had ended their regulation 72 holes on 13 under par 275.

The latter triumph was all the more remarkable considering it came on the back of a barren spell for the South African which saw him miss the cut in his four previous events and proved once again just how quickly fortunes can change in golf. It also convinced him that his game and his career were back on track after the upsetting experience of his mother passing away earlier in the year.

Anthony Wall

Soren Hansen

Peter Hanson and Anders Hansen

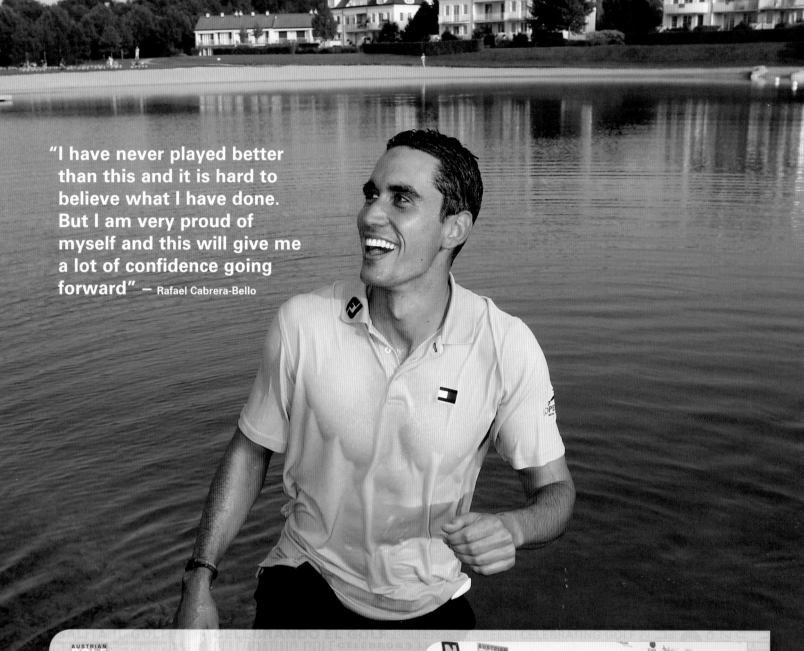

"I have never played better than this and it is hard to believe what I have done. But I am very proud of myself and this will give me a lot of confidence going forward" — Rafael Cabrera-Bello

AUSTRIAN GOLF OPEN
Fontana Golf Club
Vienna, Austria
September 17-20, 2009

1	**RAFAEL CABRERA-BELLO**		71	67	66	60	264	-20
2	Benn Barham		63	66	67	69	265	-19
3	Søren Hansen		67	67	65	68	267	-17
4	Richard Bland		68	70	65	66	269	-15
5	Louis Oosthuizen		69	67	65	69	270	-14
6	Seve Benson		69	68	68	66	271	-13
	Richard Green		65	66	69	71	271	-13
	Pablo Martin		66	68	70	67	271	-13
	Simon Wakefield		68	70	67	66	271	-13
10	David Dixon		68	67	71	66	272	-12
	Pelle Edberg		68	65	71	68	272	-12
	David Horsey		67	67	71	67	272	-12
	Damien McGrane		71	67	67	67	272	-12

LR Mag. Petra Bohuslav, Secretary of Sports for the Government of Lower Austria and Rafael Cabrera-Bello

Total Prize Fund €989,970   **First Prize** €166,660

Louis Oosthuizen

Markus Brier

Richard Green

Exclusive Club

There are many ways to win a tournament on The European Tour but, until events unfolded at the Fontana Golf Club, only Jamie Spence and Ian Woosnam had carded a 60 in the final round to do so. Now, though, Rafael Cabrera-Bello's name can be added to this exclusive club following a sensational ending to the Austrian Golf Open.

Starting the final day in a share of seventh place and eight shots adrift of Benn Barham, who had led throughout following his opening day 63, most observers believed if there were to be a maiden triumph, it would be claimed by the

Englishman and not the distant Spaniard. Cabrera-Bello, however, had other ideas.

Five birdies saw him to the turn in 30 as Barham turned in 36 and suddenly the contest was alive. Five further birdies from the tenth to the 16th saw the 25 year old from the Canary Islands reach the last with a 30 foot eagle putt for the first 59 in official European Tour competition. It stayed agonisingly above ground but the tap in birdie saw him set the target of 20 under par 264. It says much for Barham's resilience that he kept battling and indeed faced a birdie putt on the same green minutes later to force a play-off. It missed, to ensure Cabrera-Bello's place in history.

AUSTRIAN GOLF OPEN 2009

FONTANA

FONTANA

Benn Barham

vivendi trophy
WITH SEVERIANO BALLESTEROS

THE VIVENDI TROPHY WITH SEVE BALLESTEROS

Saint-Nom-la-Bretèche Golf Club
Paris, France
September 24–27, 2009

"I had a brilliant bunch of lads, every single one of them. We had great team meetings, we had a lot of energy and we had a plan from when we got here. We stuck to that plan and we came through in the end against a very strong Continental European Team"

— Paul McGinley

vivendi trophy
WITH SEVERIANO BALLESTEROS

CONTINENTAL EUROPE (Captain: Thomas Björn)		GREAT BRITAIN AND IRELAND (Captain: Paul McGinley)	
Thursday: Fourballs			
S Kjeldsen (DEN) & A Quiros (ESP)	0	G McDowell (NIR) & R McIlroy (NIR) (4 and 3)	1
H Stenson (SWE) & R Karlsson (SWE)	0	C Wood (ENG) & A Wall (ENG) (6 and 5)	1
S Hansen (DEN) & P Hanson (SWE)	0	S Dyson (ENG) & O Wilson (ENG) (3 and 2)	1
A Hansen (DEN) & F Molinari (ITA) (4 and 3)	1	R Rock (ENG) & S Webster (ENG)	0
M A Jiménez (ESP) & G Fernandez-Castaño (ESP) (2 and 1)	1	R Fisher (ENG) & N Dougherty (ENG)	0
Session Score:	**2**		**3**
Match Position:	**2**		**3**
Friday: Fourballs			
H Stenson & A Quiros	0	S Dyson & O Wilson (2 and 1)	1
P Hanson & S Hansen	0	N Dougherty & R Fisher (3 and 2)	1
A Hansen & F Molinari (3 and 1)	1	G McDowell & R McIlroy	0
G Fernandez-Castaño & R Karlsson (1 hole)	1	R Rock & S Webster	0
M A Jiménez & S Kjeldsen	0	A Wall & C Wood (3 and 2)	1
Session Score:	**2**		**3**
Match Position:	**4**		**6**
Saturday Morning: Greensomes			
H Stenson & P Hanson	0	R McIlroy & G McDowell (2 and 1)	1
R Karlsson & G Fernandez-Castaño	0	R Rock & N Dougherty (5 and 4)	1
A Hansen & F Molinari	0	R Fisher & C Wood (1 hole)	1
M A Jiménez & A Quiros (1 hole)	1	S Dyson & O Wilson	0
Session Score:	**1**		**3**
Match Position:	**5**		**9**
Saturday Afternoon: Foursomes			
S Hansen & S Kjeldsen	0	R McIlroy & G McDowell (2 and 1)	1
H Stenson & P Hanson (halved)	½	N Dougherty & S Webster (halved)	½
A Hansen & F Molinari	0	R Fisher & C Wood (3 and 2)	1
A Quiros & M A Jiménez	0	R Rock & O Wilson (1 hole)	1
Session Score:	**½**		**3½**
Match Position:	**5½**		**12½**
Sunday: Singles			
H Stenson	0	R McIlroy (1 hole)	1
R Karlsson	0	G McDowell (3 and 2)	1
A Quiros (halved)	½	A Wall (halved)	½
M A Jiménez (3 and 1)	1	R Fisher	0
S Hansen (4 and 2)	1	S Webster	0
S Kjeldsen (3 and 1)	1	S Dyson	0
G Fernandez-Castaño	0	R Rock (1 hole)	1
A Hansen (7 and 6)	1	N Dougherty	0
P Hanson (halved)	½	C Wood (halved)	½
F Molinari (5 and 4)	1	O Wilson	0
Session Score:	**6**		**4**
CONTINENTAL EUROPE	**11½**	**GREAT BRITAIN AND IRELAND**	**16½**

Total Prize Fund €1,150,000   **Per player winning Team €65,000**   **Per player losing Team €50,000**

Anders Hansen

Francesco Molinari

Rory McIlroy

vivendi trophy
WITH SEVE BALLESTEROS

Cohesion and Energy

It might not be The Ryder Cup but the competition in The Vivendi Trophy with Seve Ballesteros was, at times, just as intense before the players from Great Britain and Ireland recorded their fifth straight victory in the contest over those from Continental Europe.

The biennial contest, which began life as The Seve Trophy in 2000, gives an opportunity for potential Ryder Cup hopefuls to experience team golf at the highest level in non-Ryder Cup years.

Sadly unable to be present at Saint-Nom-la-Bretèche due to his continuing recuperation after brain surgery, Ballesteros, nevertheless, was there in spirit. Before the match he spoke to respective captains Thomas Björn and Paul McGinley to wish them and their teams well, and on Sunday he sent a televised message from his home in Pedreña to all involved in the competition.

Watching at home, the great man must have been impressed not only by the quality of the golf but also by the passion shown by all the competitors. GB&I fielded four players from the top 50 of the Official World Golf Ranking compared with eight from their opponents' line-up but, when the respective prize money won by both sides

during the season was totted up, there was nothing between them.

Both captains, who could yet be involved behind the scenes as assistants to European Team Captain Colin Montgomerie in The 2010 Ryder Cup should they not make the contest themselves as players, prepared meticulously and the players responded with enthusiasm.

Although GB&I won the fourball series 3-2 on both Thursday and Friday, it was on Saturday in the morning greensomes and afternoon foursomes that the team, who had begun the week as underdogs with the bookmakers, showed cohesion and energy to take command.

From the eight points on offer on the day, McGinley's men bagged six and half which meant that going into the final ten singles on Sunday, with a 12 ½ -5 ½ point lead, they needed only two points for outright victory, a requirement reduced to one and a half when Anthony Wall pulled out with an injured shoulder meaning, under competition rules, his match with Alvaro Quiros was declared a half.

The Continental European team battled bravely on the final day and indeed, salvaged some pride when they took the

THE 2010 RYDER CUP, US OPEN, ALL WORLD GOLF CHAMPIONSHIPS, US PGA CHAMPIONSHIP, THE EUROPEAN TOUR.

FOR AN UNBEATABLE LINE-UP OF LIVE GOLF COVERAGE FROM AROUND THE WORLD
CALL 08442 411 014 OR VISIT WWW.SKYSPORTS.COM

SKY SPORTS HD

singles session by 6-4 overall to see the contest end 16 ½ - 11 ½ , incredibly the third match in a row to produce that precise GB&I winning margin. The destination of the trophy, however, was decided much earlier in the afternoon thanks to the dynamic Northern Irish duo of Graeme McDowell and Rory McIlroy.

The partnership, which must surely be considered a potential Ryder Cup one for 2010 and beyond, had won three points out of four in tandem over the previous three days and their momentum was not halted when they were separated; McIlroy claiming the scalp of World Number Five Henrik Stenson on the final green before McDowell took GB&I over the finishing line with his 3 and 2 defeat of Stenson's fellow Swede Robert Karlsson.

Thomas Björn had urged his team to play for personal pride on Sunday and individually they did just that. However, the quality of golf was outstanding from both teams; birdies and eagles aplenty on an excellent golf course with a risk-and-reward character ideally suited to match play.

Particularly memorable, from a Continental Europe perspective, was Denmark's Anders Hansen, whose ten birdies in 12 holes helped him to a thumping 7 and 6 victory over Nick Dougherty and saw him end the week with three points out of five, the best return from Björn's team alongside Spaniard Miguel Angel Jiménez and Francesco Molinari of Italy.

On the GB&I side, both McDowell and McIlroy ended the week with four points out of five but pride of place went to debutant Chris Wood, the young Englishman showing class on the course with four points out of four over the first three days, and class off the course too when he conceded Peter Hanson's six foot putt on the final green of their singles contest to halve their particular match.

The Vivendi Trophy with Seve Ballesteros was a huge success. Inspired golf and razor sharp competition was contested in superb weather on a terrific course, all of which ensured new sponsors Vivendi, and Seve himself, could not have asked for anything more.

Renton Laidlaw
The Golf Channel

Henrik Stenson and fans

Graeme McDowell

Chris Wood

ALFRED DUNHILL
LINKS CHAMPIONSHIP

ALFRED DUNHILL LINKS CHAMPIONSHIP
Old Course St Andrews, Carnoustie and Kingsbarns
Scotland
October 1-4, 2009

1	**SIMON DYSON**		**68**	**66**	**68**	**66**	**268**	**-20**
2	Rory McIlroy		68	65	69	69	271	-17
	Oliver Wilson		69	67	70	65	271	-17
4	Rafael Cabrera-Bello		70	68	65	69	272	-16
	Richie Ramsay		67	66	70	69	272	-16
6	Ross McGowan		66	68	71	68	273	-15
7	Darren Clarke		68	68	67	71	274	-14
	Luke Donald		72	65	64	73	274	-14
9	Grégory Bourdy		73	67	67	68	275	-13
	François Delamontagne		71	67	67	70	275	-13
	Kenneth Ferrie		69	66	69	71	275	-13
	Ricardo Gonzalez		70	71	68	66	275	-13
	Gary Lockerbie		69	71	67	68	275	-13
	Paul McGinley		69	67	69	70	275	-13
	Lee Westwood		73	67	66	69	275	-13

Christopher Colfer, Chief Executive Officer, Alfred Dunhill Limited and Simon Dyson

Total Prize Fund €3,242,641   **First Prize** €540,440

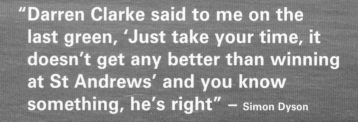

"Darren Clarke said to me on the last green, 'Just take your time, it doesn't get any better than winning at St Andrews' and you know something, he's right" — Simon Dyson

Oliver Wilson

16
423 yds 387 mtrs
Par 4
OLD COURSE

ALFRED DUNHILL
LINKS CHAMPIONSHIP
dunhill
LONDON

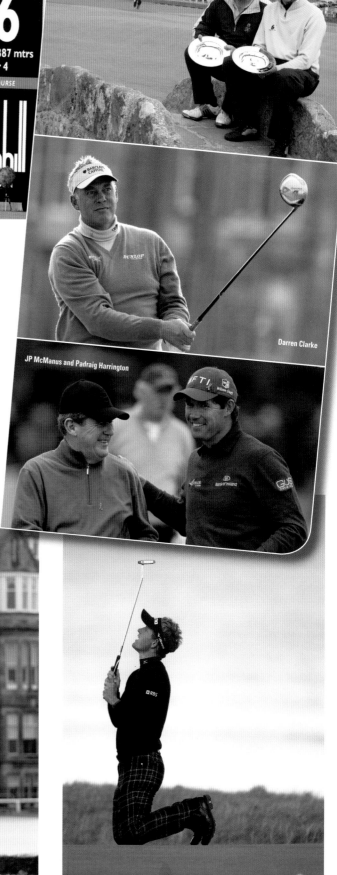

Ireland's Kieran McManus and professional Søren Hansen of Denmark, winners of the Team Event on 44 under par 244

Darren Clarke

JP McManus and Padraig Harrington

As Good as it Gets

Six weeks previously, when a closing course record 63 saw him win the KLM Open in The Netherlands; Simon Dyson admitted it had been the round of his life. After the final round in St Andrews, however, the Englishman revised his opinion.

Granted, the 66 on the Old Course was three shots more than he scored at Kennemer, but it was the manner of his play at the Home of Golf allied to the fact the victory swept him into the top 50 on the Official World Golf Ranking for the first time and into the top ten in The Race to Dubai, that left him in no doubt that this was as good as it gets.

Alongside Rory McIlroy in second place going into the last day – staged on Monday

due to all of Saturday's play being lost to high winds –Dyson immediately overhauled leader Luke Donald with a blistering start to proceedings.

The 31 year old birdied six of the first seven holes and was only a fraction of an inch away from being out in 29. Nevertheless, the birdie barrage spreadeagled the field and despite his only departures from par on the inward half being a birdie three at the 12th and a bogey five at the 17th, he still won comfortably by three shots from the fast-finishing Oliver Wilson and McIlroy, whose consolation was that he moved top of The Race to Dubai.

TEAM RESULTS

1	**SØREN HANSEN AND KIERAN MCMANUS**	63	61	61	59	244
2	Scott Strange and Steve Waugh	65	58	63	63	249
3	Marcus Fraser and John A Bryan Jr	65	63	65	59	252
	Simon Dyson and Kelly Slater	64	65	63	60	252

Richie Ramsay

Luke Donald

MADRID MASTERS
Centro Nacional de Golf
Madrid, Spain
October 8-11, 2009

Gela Alarco, Executive Vice-President of Turismo Madrid and Ross McGowan

1	**ROSS MCGOWAN**		66	66	60	71	263	-25
2	Mikko Ilonen		74	63	63	66	266	-22
3	David Drysdale		66	65	69	67	267	-21
4	Gareth Maybin		70	68	68	64	270	-18
	Gary Murphy		67	65	70	68	270	-18
	Alexander Noren		71	67	67	65	270	-18
7	Ignacio Garrido		74	63	67	67	271	-17
	Anthony Wall		66	67	70	68	271	-17
	Danny Willett		66	67	66	72	271	-17
10	Jorge Campillo		67	66	68	71	272	-16
	Emanuele Canonica		67	65	69	71	272	-16
	Luke Donald		71	69	65	67	272	-16
	Miguel Angel Jiménez		70	68	66	68	272	-16
	Gary Lockerbie		68	70	68	66	272	-16
	Michael Lorenzo-Vera		69	66	64	73	272	-16
	Fabrizio Zanotti		71	65	65	71	272	-16

Total Prize Fund €1,506,741   **First Prize** €250,000

10
PAR 5
528 YARDS
483 METERS

"I came here this week in form and it's lovely to walk away with the trophy. It means a lot to win on Tour, that's another goal of mine out of the way, and hopefully I can progress from here" — Ross McGowan

Fabrizio Zanotti

Mikko Ilonen

Vital Statistic

It is fair to say that Ross McGowan will not mind too much that his sparkling third round 60 – the round which proved the catalyst for his maiden European Tour victory – will not count in the record books due to the fact that placing was allowed on the fairways. The only statistic the 27 year old Englishman is interested in is the fact that he ended the week as number one.

Having said that, the 60 which, incredibly, featured two dropped shots, was a truly sensational effort and was the second within six weeks on Tour, following Rafael Cabrera-Bello's final round 60 to win the Austrian Golf Open in mid September.

It gave the former English Amateur champion a seven shot cushion over the field going into the final round and an eight shot lead over Mikko Ilonen who did not give up the fight. Indeed, as the birdies refused to come for McGowan, the Finn reduced the deficit to two with only four to play.

But a ten foot birdie putt for the Englishman on the 15th eased his worries and when wooden sleepers above the lake on the 18th stopped his ball from dropping into the drink, McGowan knew the title was his. Ilonen's brave 66 saw him take second, three shots adrift, with Scotland's David Drysdale in third a further shot back.

David Drysdale

> "Winning is definitely a habit and I got out of that habit. Hopefully now I have won again, I can go on to win more – I'm really looking forward to the rest of the season"
>
> — Lee Westwood

PORTUGAL MASTERS
Oceânico Victoria Golf Course
Vilamoura, Portugal
October 15–18, 2009

Lee Westwood and Frederico Costa, Vice President of Turismo de Portugal

1	**LEE WESTWOOD**		66	67	66	66	**265**	**-23**
2	Francesco Molinari		63	66	68	70	267	-21
3	Padraig Harrington		69	62	71	67	269	-19
4	Peter Hanson		71	65	66	68	270	-18
	Marcel Siem		67	69	67	67	270	-18
6	Johan Edfors		69	66	68	68	271	-17
	Retief Goosen		68	64	64	75	271	-17
	Alexander Noren		70	70	69	62	271	-17
	Justin Rose		65	70	70	66	271	-17
	Charl Schwartzel		65	65	71	70	271	-17
	Danny Willett		69	68	66	68	271	-17

Total Prize Fund €2,994,530   First Prize €500,000

Retief Goosen

Marcel Siem

Padraig Harrington

PERFECTLY PRICED

Special promotions - available now
www.visitportugal.com

Portugal
Europe's West Coast

QUADRO
DE REFERÊNCIA
ESTRATÉGICO
NACIONAL

TURISMO DE
PORTUGAL

Westwood Ho!

After three play-off defeats, two near misses in Major Championships and an astonishing 26 top ten finishes since his last victory, Lee Westwood ended more than two years without a European Tour title by capturing the Portugal Masters.

Successive weekend rounds of 66 helped the Englishman to a 23 under par total of 265 and a two shot victory over Italy's Francesco Molinari but perhaps, more importantly, the €500,000 first place cheque also saw the 36 year old move back to the top of The Race to Dubai approaching the home straight and up to fifth on the Official World Golf Ranking.

Going into the final round three shots adrift of leader Retief Goosen, Westwood knew he had to make a quick impact and did just that with birdies at each of the first four holes. With the South African slipping back, Westwood pressed on until the crucial moment arrived at the par five 17th.

His second shot finished long and left but, from 30 yards, he conjured up a magical escape through the trees, tapped in for a birdie four and parred the last for victory.

Molinari, second going into the final round, maintained that position with a closing 70 while Padraig Harrington, who had thrilled the crowds on Friday with a 62, carded a final round 67 to take third place, four shots adrift of Westwood.

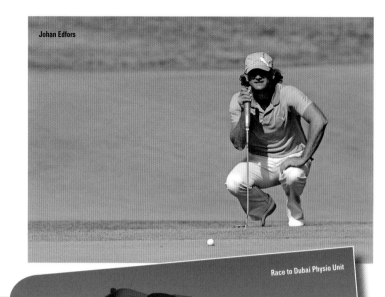
Johan Edfors

Race to Dubai Physio Unit

A cheque for €40,000 was given to SOS Children's Villages charity following the Genworth Financial 'Putts for Charity' Pro Challenge after the first round

Peter Hanson

CASTELLÓ MASTERS COSTA AZAHAR
Club de Campo del Mediterráneo
Castellon, Spain
October 22-25, 2009

1	**MICHAEL JONZON**		64	68	65	67	264	-20
2	Martin Kaymer		63	67	68	67	265	-19
	Christian Nilsson		69	66	65	65	265	-19
4	Sergio Garcia		63	68	67	69	267	-17
5	Maarten Lafeber		71	67	64	66	268	-16
6	Robert Allenby		64	66	71	68	269	-15
	Søren Hansen		70	68	65	66	269	-15
8	Darren Clarke		68	70	67	65	270	-14
	Andrew Coltart		70	64	69	67	270	-14
	Peter Hanson		66	68	66	70	270	-14
	Sam Hutsby		65	68	66	71	270	-14

L-R: Miguel Ángel Mulet, Vicepresident Diputación de Castellón, Michael Jonzon and Vicente Rambla, Vicepresident Generalitat Valenciana

Total Prize Fund €2,029,865   **First Prize** €333,330

"I am absolutely over the moon. It's going to take time for this to sink in but I am so thrilled, not only to have a playing status for next year but also for the way I handled myself this week" → Michael Jonzon

Søren Hansen

Maarten Lafeber

Martin Kaymer

Admirable Nerve

Producing a performance capable of winning a tournament on The European Tour is hard enough at the best of times; to do it when you have to is even more laudable. Which is why Michael Jonzon was rightly proud of his courageous victory in the CASTELLÓ MASTERS Costa Azahar.

Going into the week in 158th place in The Race to Dubai, securing enough money to keep his card for the 2010 season was uppermost in the mind of the 37 year old whose only previous Tour victory had come in the 1997 Portuguese Masters. Now, thanks to a glorious four days in the east of Spain, Jonzon knows exactly where he will be playing until the end of 2011.

Leading going into the final round, the Swede's understandable anxiety in the home straight was there for all to see as he double bogeyed the 15th and dropped another shot at the 17th to bring the chasing pack of Martin Kaymer, Christian Nilsson and tournament host Sergio Garcia into the picture.

But, with admirable nerve, he steadied the ship, holing from 18 feet for a birdie three at the last which saw him edge a shot ahead of Nilsson. Now only Kaymer, back from a foot injury which had seen him miss the last two months, could draw level. But, when the German missed his birdie putt from nine feet, the title, and the day, belonged to Jonzon.

Sergio Garcia

"I am always very confident and feel that I can achieve great things. I believe that if you apply yourself then there is nothing you can't achieve - I believe that more than anything" — Ian Poulter

BARCLAYS SINGAPORE OPEN
Sentosa Golf Club (Serapong Course)
Singapore
October 29-November 1, 2009

1	**IAN POULTER**		66	64	72	72	274	-10
2	Wen-chong Liang		69	68	68	70	275	-9
3	Scott Hend		72	66	69	69	276	-8
	Adam Scott		72	71	65	68	276	-8
5	Anders Hansen		68	71	68	70	277	-7
	Graeme McDowell		71	65	67	74	277	-7
	Charl Schwartzel		72	68	68	69	277	-7
8	Niclas Fasth		69	67	71	71	278	-6
9	Marcus Both		72	71	67	69	279	-5
	Andrew Dodt		69	68	70	72	279	-5
	Kodai Ichihara		68	68	71	72	279	-5
	Kenichi Kuboya		70	70	67	72	279	-5
	Thomas Levet		68	68	73	70	279	-5

Robert Morrice, Chairman and Chief Executive Asia Pacific, Barclays PLC and Ian Poulter

Total Prize Fund €3,318,713   **First Prize** €554,127

Graeme McDowell

Anders Hansen

Adam Scott

Stylish Victory

Without question, October represented the month where winning droughts were ended on The European Tour International Schedule. For the third consecutive week a player got his hands on the silverware for the first time in a while. Two weeks ago Lee Westwood won for the first time in over two years, last week Michael Jonzon ended a 12 year barren spell and now it was the turn of Ian Poulter to win on The European Tour for the first time in three years.

Not only that, the 33 year old Englishman did it in style; becoming only the third player of the 2009 season – following Rory McIlroy in the Dubai Desert Classic

and Phil Mickelson in the WGC-CA Championship – to triumph wire-to-wire.

From the moment his opening 66 put him in pole position Poulter became the man to beat in the tournament co-sanctioned with the Asian Tour for the first time. Refusing to be fazed by the many rain interruptions, Poulter continued to lead and indeed held a five stroke lead with nine holes to play.

A strong surge from the chasing pack saw his advantage cut to one standing on the 18th tee but the Englishman held his nerve and a solid par four saw him claim glory, a victory which also saw him move into the top ten on The Race to Dubai and 15th on the Official World Golf Ranking.

Liang Wen-chong

VOLVO WORLD MATCH PLAY CHAMPIONSHIP
Finca Cortesin Golf Club
Caseras, Spain
October 29-November 1, 2009

CHAMPION	ROSS FISHER	
Runner-Up	Anthony Kim	
Third	Robert Allenby	
Fourth	Angel Cabrera	

Final: Ross Fisher beat Anthony Kim 4 and 3
Consolation Final: Robert Allenby beat Angel Cabrera at the 19th hole

Total Prize Fund €3,250,000*   **First Prize** €750,000*
* Capped for The Race to Dubai €2,148,177 / €541,667

Per Ericsson, President & CEO, Volvo Event Management and Ross Fisher

"I'm absolutely ecstatic. It's been a long, gruelling week but obviously very worthwhile. The only thing missing for me this year was a win and now I've put that right" – Ross Fisher

Camilo Villegas

Perfect Match

With European Ryder Cup Captain Colin Montgomerie looking on from the sidelines it was always going to be a good time to promote your match play credentials and Ross Fisher did that better than anyone when he capped a superb week in the south of Spain with victory in the Volvo World Match Play Championship.

Not only had the tournament found itself a new sponsor and a new venue after 44 years at Wentworth Club in England, it also featured a new round robin group format in the early stages. No-one was more appreciative of that fact that Fisher himself who lost his opening match to fellow countryman Lee Westwood.

Had it been the old days, Fisher would have been packing his bags but he took advantage of the new format in style; beating Jeev

Milkha Singh and Camilo Villegas in his final two groups matches to qualify for the semi-finals where he ousted Masters Tournament Champion Angel Cabrera on the 39th green of an epic clash.

In the final he faced Anthony Kim who also lost his opening match before recovering to oust Robert Allenby 5 and 4 in the semi-final. In The 2008 Ryder Cup at Valhalla, Kim had been one of America's star performers and indeed was trying to become the youngest winner in the tournament's history.

But from the moment he lost the opening hole, he was never in front. Fisher remained one up at lunch and gradually pulled away in the afternoon round before bringing the curtain down on the 15th green by 4 and 3.

Anthony Kim

Lee Westwood

Angel Cabrera and Robert Allenby

WGC - HSBC CHAMPIONS
Sheshan International Golf Club
Shanghai, China
November 5-8, 2009

1	**PHIL MICKELSON**		69	66	67	69	**271**	**-17**
2	Ernie Els		70	71	68	63	272	-16
3	Ryan Moore		66	69	70	68	273	-15
4	Rory McIlroy		73	68	70	63	274	-14
5	Nick Watney		64	70	70	71	275	-13
6	Martin Kaymer		66	74	69	67	276	-12
	Tiger Woods		67	67	70	72	276	-12
8	Alvaro Quiros		69	66	76	66	277	-11
	Lee Westwood		70	71	65	71	277	-11
10	Retief Goosen		71	71	68	68	278	-10
	Anthony Kim		67	69	72	70	278	-10
	Søren Kjeldsen		69	72	71	66	278	-10
	Daisuke Maruyama		72	69	74	63	278	-10
	Francesco Molinari		73	67	70	68	278	-10
	Geoff Ogilvy		72	74	65	67	278	-10
	Pat Perez		68	69	75	66	278	-10

Phil Mickelson and Sandy Flockhart, Chief Executive Officer, HSBC Asia-Pacific

Total Prize Fund €4,694,030   **First Prize** €807,575

"It feels terrific to have won this tournament. It has been very special to have had a World Golf Championship event here in China and to be champion of it, is just great" — Phil Mickelson

Ernie Els

HSBC Hexagon Suite

Lee Westwood

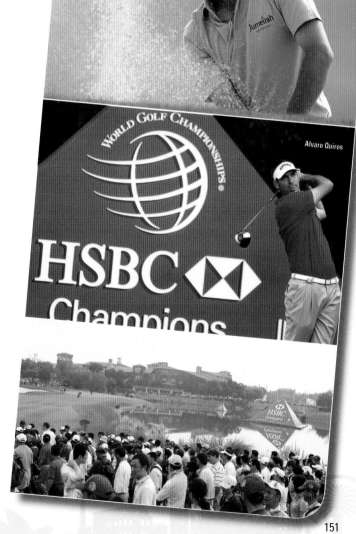

Rory McIlroy

Alvaro Quiros

Curtain Call

It is fair to say there cannot be a more perfect way to bring the curtain down on your 2009 golfing season than what Phil Mickelson achieved in the WGC-HSBC Champions.

Always popular in China, the left hander arrived in Shanghai eager to promote his upcoming course design project and teaching academy in Tian Jin near Beijing. What better way to do that to triumph in front of an adoring public who took him to their hearts two years ago when he won the event for the first time?

Going into the final round with a two shot lead over Tiger Woods and Nick Watney, the world licked its lips in anticipation of a thrilling head-to-head between the Number One and Two players in the world. The only problem was, no-one appeared to have given Woods a copy of that particular script.

An error-strewn opening saw him reach the turn in 39 and although he rallied to finish tied sixth, he was never a threat to Mickelson.

Instead, that came from a resurgent Ernie Els who stormed to the turn in 30 and notched four more birdies on the inward half only to rue a trip into the water at the last which cost him a bogey six. It left Mickelson needing a par five to win and although he flirted with the rough, he succeeded.

American Ryan Moore took third a shot clear of the fast finishing Rory McIlroy who matched Els' 63 to help him move second on The Race to Dubai. Lee Westwood took eighth place to stay ahead with €2,404,579, followed by McIlroy (€2,352,258), Martin Kaymer (€2,332,544), Ross Fisher (€2,105,046) and Paul Casey (€2,014,063), who was forced to retire after three rounds following a recurrence of his rib injury.

"I have really enjoyed myself here. I've never won in Australia before, so now I've won on every playable continent which is something I've always wanted to achieve" – Tiger Woods

JBWere MASTERS
Melbourne

JBWERE MASTERS
Kingston Heath Golf Club
Melbourne, Australia
November 12-15, 2009

1	TIGER WOODS		66	68	72	68	274	-14
2	Greg Chalmers		68	69	69	70	276	-12
3	François Delamontagne		71	70	68	69	278	-10
	Jason Dufner		70	67	71	70	278	-10
5	James Nitties		66	71	69	73	279	-9
6	Cameron Percy		67	72	69	72	280	-8
	Adam Scott		71	71	69	69	280	-8
8	Stuart Appleby		69	70	71	71	281	-7
9	Alejandro Cañizares		73	72	69	68	282	-6
	Klas Eriksson		71	73	66	72	282	-6
	Craig Scott		71	72	70	69	282	-6

Tiger Woods and the Honourable John Brumby, Premier of Victoria

Total Prize Fund €921,461   **First Prize** €173,117

François Delamontagne

Adam Scott

JBWere MASTERS Melbourne CHAMPION 2009

Seve Benson

Main Attraction

There are many words, several of them colloquial, which are part and parcel of everyday life around professional golf - and 'bouncebackability' is a good example.

Not surprisingly, it literally means the ability to regroup from something which has gone awry on the course; whether from one hole to the next or from one tournament to the next and Tiger Woods illustrated the latter category perfectly when he triumphed in the JBWere Masters.

Seven days earlier, the expected final day tussle between himself and Phil Mickelson in the WGC-HSBC Champions in Shanghai failed to materialise as Woods' lacklustre showing saw him fall down the leaderboard. Move forward a week and Woods bounced back to live up to his pre-tournament favourite billing impeccably.

Playing Down Under for the first time in 11 years, the World Number One was, unsurprisingly, the main attraction for the thousands of Australian golf fans who turned out and he did not let them down; sharing the lead after a first round 66 before becoming the fourth wire-to-wire winner of The 2009 European Tour season with subsequent rounds of 68-72-68.

Elsewhere, a full 11 shots behind Woods in a share of 17th place, was Seve Benson. The young Englishman might not have caused the merest blip on the radar of most of the spectators but his performance was noteworthy nonetheless as his cheque for €11,312 helped guarantee him 120th place on The Race to Dubai – the last player to keep his card for the 2010 season by rights.

UBS HONG KONG OPEN
Hong Kong Golf Club
Fanling, Hong Kong
November 12-15, 2009

1	**GRÉGORY BOURDY**		64	67	63	67	**261**	**-19**
2	Rory McIlroy		66	68	65	64	263	-17
3	Robert-Jan Derksen		63	68	65	68	264	-16
	Francesco Molinari		66	68	66	64	264	-16
5	Raphaël Jacquelin		66	68	68	64	266	-14
	Ian Poulter		68	66	68	64	266	-14
7	Peter Lawrie		66	68	66	67	267	-13
8	Simon Dyson		68	67	67	66	268	-12
9	David Dixon		64	69	69	67	269	-11
	Scott Strange		68	65	70	66	269	-11

Grégory Bourdy and Allen Lo, CEO Hong Kong Branch UBS AG

Total Prize Fund €1,658,956   **First Prize** €279,289

"This is fantastic. It is my mother's birthday today so I dedicate this to her. I needed the win to get to Dubai and I've done it – this was simply a week where everything went right"

— Grégory Bourdy

Rory McIlroy

Francesco Molinari

Special Success

It might have Orwellian overtones but there is no denying the fact that, while every win on The European Tour International Schedule is special, some are more special than others. For Grégory Bourdy, that was particularly true of his success in the UBS Hong Kong Open.

Not only did his superb all round display see him become the first Frenchman to win tournaments in three consecutive years on Tour, he also completed the triumph on his mother Martine's 57th birthday. Finally, the victory saw him move from 86th to 47th on The Race to Dubai and thus guarantee him a place in next week's Dubai World Championship.

Bourdy's gain was Stephen Dodd's loss as the Welshman, who missed the cut, dropped from 59th place at the start of the week to 62nd place and out of the field for the season-ending event. Sharing Dodd's misfortune was Darren Clarke who battled bravely to a share of 11th place in Fanling but found it only good enough to move him from 63rd to 61st – one place and a mere €7,381 short of booking his place in Dubai.

Bourdy held off the challenge of Rory McIlroy to claim the title and while the Northern Irishman was disappointed not to win, the blow was cushioned by the fact he moved back to the top of The Race to Dubai, some €128,173 ahead of the man he leapfrogged, England's Lee Westwood, who could do no better than a share of 54th place.

Robert-Jan Derksen

Ian Poulter

Totally Focused

DUBAI
WORLD CHAMPIONSHIP
PRESENTED BY DP WORLD

DUBAI WORLD CHAMPIONSHIP PRESENTED BY: DP WORLD
Earth Course, Jumeirah Golf Estates
Dubai, United Arab Emirates
November 19-22, 2009

1	**LEE WESTWOOD**		66	69	66	64	265	-23
2	Ross McGowan		71	66	66	68	271	-17
3	Rory McIlroy		68	69	69	67	273	-15
4	Padraig Harrington		68	69	69	68	274	-14
	Geoff Ogilvy		70	69	68	67	274	-14
6	Alexander Noren		70	69	67	69	275	-13
7	Sergio Garcia		71	67	69	69	276	-12
	Adam Scott		68	73	67	68	276	-12
9	Peter Hanson		72	71	66	69	278	-10
	Miguel Angel Jiménez		72	68	69	69	278	-10
	Ian Poulter		71	74	68	65	278	-10

Lee Westwood and His Excellency Matar al Tayer, Vice President, Dubai Sports Council

Total Prize Fund €4,955,642   **First Prize** €830,675

"That felt pretty good I have to say. It's hard to imagine playing better, getting the breaks when you need them, and I also didn't think I'd feel so calm out there. I learned a lot from my Open experience this year, tried to put it into practise, and today it paid off" — Lee Westwood

When Rory McIlroy was asked to predict a winning score in the eagerly anticipated inaugural Dubai World Championship presented by: DP World, he thought carefully and then gave his answer. "Mid-teens, 14 or 15 under par," said the 20 year old.

Ross Fisher raised his eyebrows on being told that soon afterwards and commented: "I'd love mid-teens. I think if you can break 70 every day, you'd have a pretty decent score."

The Greg Norman-designed Earth course at Jumeirah Golf Estates was, at 7,675 yards, the second longest layout in European Tour history and with its large white bunkers, water hazards and undulating greens there were those thinking that double figures would be no mean achievement, especially given what was at stake.

Not only was there a tournament purse of US$7.5million on offer, but also a bonus pool of the same amount for the top 15 finishers in The Race to Dubai. Never before in Tour history had an event offered up the possibility of a putt being potentially worth a combined US$2.75million come the end of the week and, in truth, nobody knew quite what to expect from the 58 players on view.

It quickly became apparent, however, that no-one had appraised Lee Westwood of such concerns.

With Paul Casey unable to make the trip after suffering a recurrence of his rib muscle injury during the WGC-HSBC Champions in Shanghai, there were four players left in the race to be The European Tour Number One for the 2009 season - Martin Kaymer, Fisher, McIlroy and Westwood.

McIlroy's fourth place in Shanghai and his runners-up finish in the UBS Hong Kong Open had put him in the driving seat. But such were the amounts now on offer that victory for Westwood or Kaymer would give them The Race to Dubai title as well, while Fisher knew he stood a good chance too if he could emulate his winning performance at the Volvo World Match Play Championship less than a month earlier.

Fisher and Kaymer, however, were unable to propel themselves into the reckoning. So the spotlight focused on the two International Sports Management stablemates - one trying to become the youngest Order of Merit champion since Seve Ballesteros in 1976; the other trying to recapture the crown he held in 2000.

They went head-to-head on the opening day and, with a six under par 66, Westwood outscored McIlroy by two. Australian Robert Allenby led with a 65 but Westwood shared second place with Colombia's Camilo Villegas and Chris Wood of England.

Westwood swooped ahead with a second round of 69 - not that he knew it until he had completed his day's work. Under new instructions from caddie Billy Foster, he was ignoring all leaderboards for the first time in his career - and at the halfway point, with a two stroke advantage ahead of Padraig Harrington, Ross McGowan, Louis Oosthuizen, Allenby, McIlroy and Villegas, there was no reason to change that philosophy.

It had been an amazing second round of twists and turns, with McIlroy initially taking over as front runner, only for Harrington to move into pole position before a seven on the hazardous 620 yard 18th cost him a share of the lead.

After 15 holes of the third round McIlroy and Westwood shared the lead. McIlroy, however, finished with three bogeys after he – like Harrington the day before – found the water on the last.

Westwood made no such mistakes. He carved out a brilliant 66 to stay two ahead of McGowan, who scored a second successive 66, and five in front of Sweden's Alexander Noren, Harrington and McIlroy.

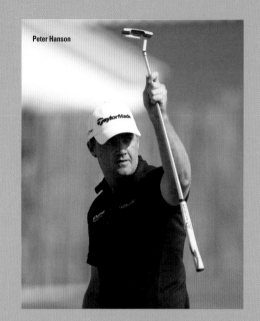
Peter Hanson

Rory McIlroy and Geoff Ogil

The four men – at the start of the week – who had the chance to win The Race to Dubai: Martin Kaymer, Lee Westwood, Rory McIlroy and Ross Fisher.

"Look at the leaderboard and tell me anybody else that has won 30 tournaments. I finish off tournaments more than most people on that leaderboard as well. I know what to do when the time comes," said Westood.

True to his word Westwood, totally focused and oozing confidence, birdied five of the first seven holes and after another on the tenth was suddenly an amazing seven strokes clear. Furthermore, despite McGowan having five successive back nine birdies and McIlroy producing five in six holes from the ninth, there was no way the 36 year old from Worksop was going to give them even a sniff of victory.

For McGowan there was good reason to smile as he shook Westwood's hand on the 18th green. He had followed his maiden win in the Madrid Masters little more than a month earlier on The

European Tour International Schedule with another outstanding performance. He had also climbed to number 12 in The Race to Dubai.

Westwood, however, had won the Dubai World Championship and The Race to Dubai. His final putt on the Earth course confirmed a first prize cheque of US$1,250,000 and a further US$1,500,000 from the Bonus Pool for finishing Number One over the course of the season. The US$2,750,000 marked golf's single largest prize fund paid to a single player on The European Tour.

Westwood was understandably moved to tears moments after stepping from the recorder's hut. He called it the greatest display of his career and one made all the sweeter for the fact that he had fallen from fourth on the Official World Golf Ranking in 2001 to

Ross McGowan

Below Wives and partners of competitors in the Dubai World Championship presented a cheque for $50,000, on behalf of The Tour Players' Foundation, to the Special Needs Families Group in Dubai

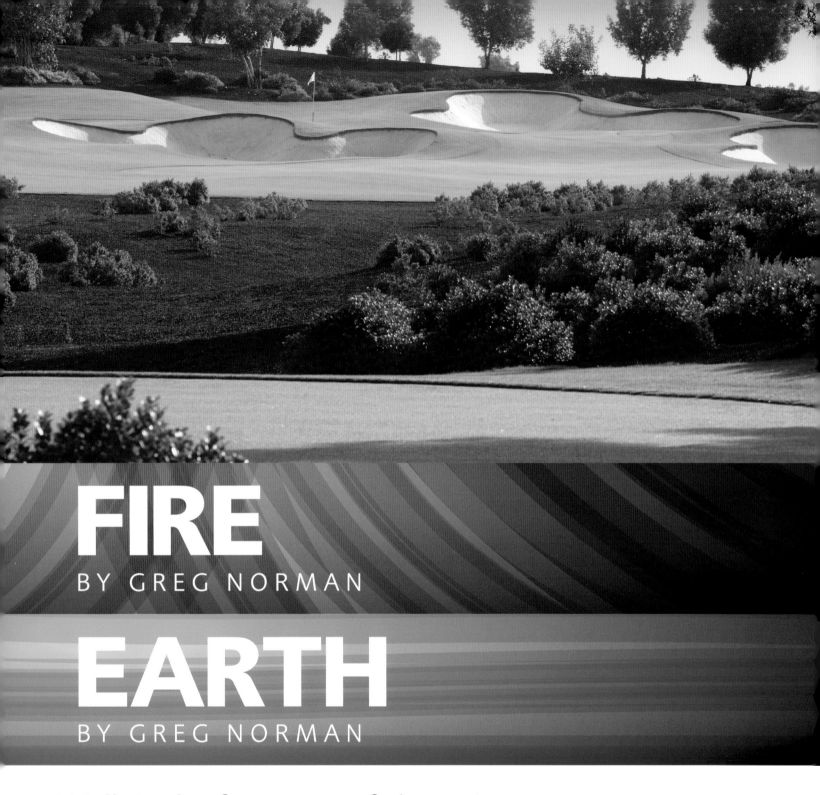

FIRE
BY GREG NORMAN

EARTH
BY GREG NORMAN

Walk in the footsteps of champions.

Tee off at Jumeirah Golf Estates, home of the Dubai World Championship.

At the Dubai World Championship, golf's greatest names went head to head on Greg Norman's newest masterpiece – the magnificent Earth course. Join "The Club" at Jumeirah Golf Estates and you can follow in their footsteps, becoming one of the privileged few to play Earth, and the equally stunning Fire course. Limited memberships are now available. For information and to apply, email membership@jumeirahgolfestates.com or call +971 4 363 0519 today.

JUMEIRAHGOLFESTATES.COM

outside the top 250 little more than a year later. He was now back up to fourth. "To drop completely into obscurity, I suppose, and then to come back and crown it all by winning this obviously means a lot," he said. "I'd have to say it's better than 2000. I'm much more mature now. I've got a more rounded game, I think. There's less flaws, there's less weaknesses. I was calm all week. I was surprised how calm I was today. I was very confident in what I was doing.

"It's a fantastic tournament. If you ever wanted a tournament to burst on to the scene – that's probably as good as it gets out here. You've got The Race to Dubai and the two people that are in the frame for winning it coming down the stretch. You probably couldn't get any better.

"I think Dubai and the golf course and The European Tour have come out of it looking fantastic. I think it's a great effort for golf in this region. I think it's a great advert for golf on The European Tour. It shows the quality of the players we have."

He also had words for McIlroy although his comments were laced with the famous laid back and laconic wit which make him such a favourite with everyone on Tour. "What's he got going for him? Twenty years old, millionaire already, hits it miles, drives a Lamborghini and has a nice-looking girlfriend. Yeah it's hard, isn't it! Seriously though, he's had a fantastic year and he is a great talent."

In fact McIlroy, true to his pre-tournament prediction, had posted a 15 under par total. McGowan had edged him for second place on 17 under par, but when Lee Westwood finally looked at and digested the Dubai World Championship leaderboard he saw what the huge crowds had witnessed all week – a fabulous set of scores: 66-69-66-64 and a 23 under par total of 265. The moment, and the year, belonged to him.

Mark Garrod
Press Association

Sergio Garcia

Right The connection between the past and present on The European Tour was celebrated with a special presentation to Harry Vardon's son, Peter, by European Tour Chief Executive George O'Grady

Padraig Harrington and Alex Noren

Pos	Name	Country	Played	€	Pos	Name	Country	Played	€	Pos	Name	Country	Played	€
1	Lee WESTWOOD	(ENG)	(26)	4237762.07	51	James KINGSTON	(RSA)	(24)	638959.78	101	Andrew MCLARDY	(RSA)	(21)	323391.12
2	Rory MCILROY	(NIR)	(25)	3610020.29	52	Justin ROSE	(ENG)	(14)	633769.11	102	Stephen AMES	(CAN)	(6)	322939.80
3	Martin KAYMER	(GER)	(20)	2864342.29	53	Gareth MAYBIN	(NIR)	(29)	625875.70	103	Alastair FORSYTH	(SCO)	(27)	320328.80
4	Ross FISHER	(ENG)	(22)	2531183.22	54	Wen-chong LIANG	(CHN)	(15)	622347.85	104	Paul MCGINLEY	(IRL)	(26)	302433.17
5	Paul CASEY	(ENG)	(14)	2362946.92	55	Luke DONALD	(ENG)	(12)	617649.05	105	Mark FOSTER	(ENG)	(30)	301887.17
6	Geoff OGILVY	(AUS)	(13)	2202813.96	56	Niclas FASTH	(SWE)	(31)	612746.29	106	François DELAMONTAGNE	(FRA)	(28)	299733.26
7	Oliver WILSON	(ENG)	(25)	2010158.23	57	Bradley DREDGE	(WAL)	(29)	612378.47	107	David DIXON	(ENG)	(29)	295472.21
8	Simon DYSON	(ENG)	(32)	1807752.59	58	Danny WILLETT	(ENG)	(27)	596461.73	108	Gary LOCKERBIE	(ENG)	(30)	289460.64
9	Ian POULTER	(ENG)	(15)	1773469.68	59	Jamie DONALDSON	(WAL)	(29)	594696.43	109	Markus BRIER	(AUT)	(28)	286308.57
10	Sergio GARCIA	(ESP)	(17)	1660787.79	60	Damien MCGRANE	(IRL)	(32)	563128.26	110	Richard FINCH	(ENG)	(28)	284311.28
11	Ernie ELS	(RSA)	(17)	1571576.98	61	Darren CLARKE	(NIR)	(24)	534733.32	111	Sam LITTLE	(ENG)	(29)	280930.08
12	Ross McGOWAN	(ENG)	(30)	1558807.77	62	Stephen DODD	(WAL)	(25)	529929.40	112	Richard BLAND	(ENG)	(26)	277461.83
13	Søren KJELDSEN	(DEN)	(26)	1529252.92	63	Fabrizio ZANOTTI	(PAR)	(24)	511756.21	113	Shiv KAPUR	(IND)	(30)	269328.34
14	Francesco MOLINARI	(ITA)	(27)	1505010.13	64	Jeppe HULDAHL	(DEN)	(29)	510380.61	114	Mark BROWN	(NZL)	(30)	269117.04
15	Padraig HARRINGTON	(IRL)	(16)	1468232.38	65	Ignacio GARRIDO	(ESP)	(29)	502658.60	115	Paul WARING	(ENG)	(25)	265240.96
16	Peter HANSON	(SWE)	(27)	1288434.14	66	Christian CÉVAËR	(FRA)	(27)	496461.92	116	Chapchai NIRAT	(THA)	(26)	263776.79
17	Gonzalo FDEZ-CASTAÑO	(ESP)	(26)	1209372.06	67	Robert-Jan DERKSEN	(NED)	(25)	491336.92	117	Rory SABBATINI	(RSA)	(13)	261827.14
18	Henrik STENSON	(SWE)	(21)	1187231.93	68	Oskar HENNINGSSON	(SWE)	(23)	476090.33	118	Pablo MARTIN	(ESP)	(32)	254637.18
19	Thongchai JAIDEE	(THA)	(27)	1161465.90	69	Michael JONZON	(SWE)	(32)	475537.81	119	Kenneth FERRIE	(ENG)	(26)	253572.27
20	Alvaro QUIROS	(ESP)	(26)	1120472.39	70	Tim CLARK	(RSA)	(10)	471279.01	120	Seve BENSON	(ENG)	(28)	250786.15
21	Robert ALLENBY	(AUS)	(14)	1118025.04	71	Rodney PAMPLING	(AUS)	(13)	461843.62	121	Jean-François LUCQUIN	(FRA)	(32)	242403.92
22	Søren HANSEN	(DEN)	(26)	1112252.54	72	Ricardo GONZALEZ	(ARG)	(26)	442747.50	122	Andrew COLTART	(SCO)	(30)	236638.89
23	Miguel Angel JIMÉNEZ	(ESP)	(28)	1082937.08	73	Marcus FRASER	(AUS)	(26)	436921.31	123	Boo WEEKLEY	(USA)	(9)	235342.67
24	Anders HANSEN	(DEN)	(25)	1077949.97	74	Richard GREEN	(AUS)	(20)	432904.41	124	Gary MURPHY	(IRL)	(34)	234843.83
25	Alexander NOREN	(SWE)	(25)	1040143.88	75	Prayad MARKSAENG	(THA)	(18)	425637.72	125	Oliver FISHER	(ENG)	(32)	234458.56
26	Charl SCHWARTZEL	(RSA)	(25)	983622.45	76	David HORSEY	(ENG)	(27)	424666.40	126	Alessandro TADINI	(ITA)	(29)	232759.42
27	Retief GOOSEN	(RSA)	(18)	970851.37	77	Daniel VANCSIK	(ARG)	(29)	398821.94	127	Simon KHAN	(ENG)	(29)	227887.50
28	Thomas LEVET	(FRA)	(26)	902101.92	78	Rafa ECHENIQUE	(ARG)	(30)	397987.32	128	Scott DRUMMOND	(SCO)	(32)	225533.23
29	Robert ROCK	(ENG)	(26)	889397.24	79	Marcel SIEM	(GER)	(30)	393529.85	129	Scott HEND	(AUS)	(11)	221423.28
30	Camilo VILLEGAS	(COL)	(13)	886287.57	80	Felipe AGUILAR	(CHI)	(29)	389204.23	130	Alejandro CAÑIZARES	(ESP)	(26)	216910.21
31	Louis OOSTHUIZEN	(RSA)	(28)	867333.61	81	Gary ORR	(SCO)	(20)	380681.99	131	Michael LORENZO-VERA	(FRA)	(29)	214282.51
32	Johan EDFORS	(SWE)	(28)	862857.04	82	Paul LAWRIE	(SCO)	(24)	379258.14	132	Pelle EDBERG	(SWE)	(34)	213652.50
33	Graeme MCDOWELL	(NIR)	(23)	848571.36	83	Anthony KANG	(USA)	(22)	375372.63	133	Benn BARHAM	(ENG)	(28)	212587.09
34	Jeev Milkha SINGH	(IND)	(22)	847843.83	84	Marc WARREN	(SCO)	(28)	369260.87	134	Callum MACAULAY	(SCO)	(23)	210991.11
35	Nick DOUGHERTY	(ENG)	(27)	833713.24	85	Paul BROADHURST	(ENG)	(28)	365353.31	135	Marc CAYEUX	(ZIM)	(22)	210408.41
36	Adam SCOTT	(AUS)	(13)	809185.02	86	Pablo LARRAZÁBAL	(ESP)	(33)	356473.41	136	Lee SLATTERY	(ENG)	(32)	205704.51
37	Raphaël JACQUELIN	(FRA)	(30)	801280.63	87	Colin MONTGOMERIE	(SCO)	(25)	354303.90	137	Miles TUNNICLIFF	(ENG)	(28)	200525.31
38	Anthony KIM	(USA)	(12)	759291.95	88	Martin ERLANDSSON	(SWE)	(27)	352073.06	138	Grégory HAVRET	(FRA)	(29)	194981.40
39	Rafael CABRERA-BELLO	(ESP)	(32)	744296.85	89	David LYNN	(ENG)	(27)	351164.72	139	Jean-Baptiste GONNET	(FRA)	(29)	194557.81
40	Anthony WALL	(ENG)	(26)	741897.22	90	Christian NILSSON	(SWE)	(17)	343763.26	140	Stuart APPLEBY	(AUS)	(10)	193385.34
41	Scott STRANGE	(AUS)	(28)	727480.60	91	Thomas BJÖRN	(DEN)	(21)	343220.46	141	Carlos DEL MORAL	(ESP)	(26)	189232.78
42	Richard STERNE	(RSA)	(21)	708883.87	92	Mikko ILONEN	(FIN)	(28)	342238.66	142	Klas ERIKSSON	(SWE)	(25)	186980.15
43	Peter LAWRIE	(IRL)	(29)	682096.90	93	Michael HOEY	(NIR)	(26)	341326.71	143	Magnus A CARLSSON	(SWE)	(31)	185871.90
44	Chris WOOD	(ENG)	(25)	679559.28	94	Tano GOYA	(ARG)	(26)	338938.90	144	Mikael LUNDBERG	(SWE)	(27)	181845.14
45	Grégory BOURDY	(FRA)	(30)	671376.25	95	José Manuel LARA	(ESP)	(31)	334320.96	145	John DALY	(USA)	(13)	178240.33
46	Thomas AIKEN	(RSA)	(22)	660321.99	96	Maarten LAFEBER	(NED)	(31)	334270.97	146	Robert DINWIDDIE	(ENG)	(30)	170185.56
47	Steve WEBSTER	(ENG)	(26)	654551.18	97	Richie RAMSAY	(SCO)	(30)	331170.69	147	John BICKERTON	(ENG)	(25)	168376.54
48	David DRYSDALE	(SCO)	(27)	651633.56	98	Robert KARLSSON	(SWE)	(13)	329389.56	148	Branden GRACE	(RSA)	(26)	166137.68
49	Graeme STORM	(ENG)	(30)	649875.09	99	Brett RUMFORD	(AUS)	(29)	329133.75	149	Roope KAKKO	(FIN)	(12)	157145.34
50	Peter HEDBLOM	(SWE)	(29)	648873.77	100	Jyoti RANDHAWA	(IND)	(26)	324176.44	150	Jarmo SANDELIN	(SWE)	(29)	156042.70

Pos	Name	Country	Played	€
151	Steven O'HARA	(SCO)	(25)	154197.53
152	Hennie OTTO	(RSA)	(24)	151972.77
153	Shane LOWRY	(IRL)	(19)	144843.42
154	Joakim HAEGGMAN	(SWE)	(22)	142800.27
155	Phillip ARCHER	(ENG)	(32)	141831.52
156	David HOWELL	(ENG)	(29)	141489.93
157	Carl PETTERSSON	(SWE)	(6)	135249.30
158	José Maria OLAZÁBAL	(ESP)	(16)	132285.38
159	Mardan MAMAT	(SIN)	(10)	118318.87
160	José-Filipe LIMA	(POR)	(11)	118126.67
161	Terry PILKADARIS	(AUS)	(13)	111300.69
162	Peter O'MALLEY	(AUS)	(23)	110957.16
163	Andrew DODT	(AUS)	(7)	110847.62
164	Danny LEE	(NZL)	(13)	110542.81
165	Alan MCLEAN	(SCO)	(15)	105352.58
166	Wade ORMSBY	(AUS)	(24)	104871.23
167	Mads VIBE-HASTRUP	(DEN)	(30)	100123.57
168	Chris DOAK	(SCO)	(22)	99910.67
169	Chih-bing LAM	(SIN)	(12)	99625.39
170	James KAMTE	(RSA)	(16)	97483.19
171	Marcus HIGLEY	(ENG)	(18)	96615.55
172	Bernd WIESBERGER	(AUT)	(22)	94750.26
173	Åke NILSSON	(SWE)	(20)	93396.97
174	Simon WAKEFIELD	(ENG)	(33)	93223.56
175	Rhys DAVIES	(WAL)	(11)	92426.10
176	Seung-yul NOH	(KOR)	(9)	91292.25
177	Garth MULROY	(RSA)	(7)	91277.13
178	Tony CAROLAN	(AUS)	(10)	90974.91
179	Santiago LUNA	(ESP)	(14)	89829.77
180	Sam HUTSBY	(ENG)	(5)	87974.48
181	Patrik SJÖLAND	(SWE)	(15)	87969.42
182	Wil BESSELING	(NED)	(23)	87094.69
183	Inder VAN WEERELT	(NED)	(21)	85174.91
184	John E MORGAN	(ENG)	(16)	82889.33
185	S S P CHOWRASIA	(IND)	(22)	78113.19
186	Barry LANE	(ENG)	(24)	78032.00
187	Keith HORNE	(RSA)	(11)	75993.25
188	Fredrik ANDERSSON HED	(SWE)	(13)	75151.45
189	Alvaro VELASCO	(ESP)	(27)	73673.06
190	Adam BLYTH	(AUS)	(10)	73561.28
191	David GLEESON	(AUS)	(13)	73006.66
192	Iain STEEL	(MAS)	(9)	72623.14
193	David FROST	(RSA)	(20)	70732.05
194	Matthew MILLAR	(AUS)	(18)	68582.78
195	Taco REMKES	(NED)	(31)	66177.61
196	Julien CLÉMENT	(SUI)	(5)	65770.00
197	Thaworn WIRATCHANT	(THA)	(8)	65542.06
198	Phillip PRICE	(WAL)	(24)	61679.46
199	Emanuele CANONICA	(ITA)	(15)	59753.29
200	Edoardo MOLINARI	(ITA)	(6)	59595.00

FLAGS OF THE WORLD

	Abu Dhabi		Kazakhstan
	Argentina		Kenya
	Australia		Malaysia
	Austria		Morocco
	Barbados		Netherlands
	Belgium		New Zealand
	Brunei		Northern Ireland
	Chile		Norway
	China		Paraguay
	Chinese Taipei		Phillipines
	Colombia		Poland
	Czech Republic		Portugal
	Denmark		Qatar
	Dubai		Russia
	England		Scotland
	Estonia		Singapore
	Fiji		South Africa
	Finland		South Korea
	France		Spain
	Germany		Sweden
	Hong Kong		Switzerland
	Iceland		Taiwan
	India		Thailand
	Indonesia		Trinidad & Tobago
	Ireland		United Arab Emirates
	Italy		USA
	Jamaica		Wales
	Japan		Zimbabwe

Stroke Average

Pos	Name	Stroke Average	Total Strokes	Total Rounds	Pos	Name	Stroke Average	Total Strokes	Total Rounds	Pos	Name	Stroke Average	Total Strokes	Total Rounds
1	**Rory MCILROY**	**69.51**	**6256**	**90**	51	Johan EDFORS	70.92	6950	98	78	Chris WOOD	71.33	6134	86
2	Sergio GARCIA	69.83	4050	58	52	Geoff OGILVY	70.95	3122	44	80	Grégory BOURDY	71.34	6991	98
3	Francesco MOLINARI	69.85	7055	101	53	Andrew DODT	70.96	1703	24	81	James KINGSTON	71.36	5495	77
4	Paul CASEY	69.92	2727	39	54	Thomas AIKEN	70.97	4968	70	82	Christian NILSSON	71.37	3497	49
5	Lee WESTWOOD	70.00	6580	94	54	Anthony KIM	70.97	2555	36	83	Ricardo GONZALEZ	71.39	5426	76
5	Martin KAYMER	70.00	4620	66	56	Thomas LEVET	71.00	6745	95	84	Brett RUMFORD	71.41	6570	92
7	Charl SCHWARTZEL	70.06	6235	89	56	Richard STERNE	71.00	4544	64	84	David DIXON	71.41	5856	82
8	Ian POULTER	70.20	3791	54	58	Colin MONTGOMERIE	71.02	6179	87	86	John DALY	71.42	2214	31
9	Anders HANSEN	70.25	5901	84	59	Damien MCGRANE	71.05	7531	106	87	Andrew MCLARDY	71.43	4786	67
10	Retief GOOSEN	70.26	4075	58	60	Rafael CABRERA-BELLO	71.09	7393	104	87	Henrik STENSON	71.43	5000	70
10	Alexander NOREN	70.26	5972	85	61	Niclas FASTH	71.10	7039	99	89	José Manuel LARA	71.44	6287	88
12	Padraig HARRINGTON	70.33	3798	54	61	David HORSEY	71.10	6612	93	90	Shiv KAPUR	71.45	6288	88
13	Robert ALLENBY	70.34	3095	44	63	Darren CLARKE	71.11	5973	84	91	Paul MCGINLEY	71.46	6003	84
14	Miguel Angel JIMÉNEZ	70.36	7177	102	63	Marcus FRASER	71.11	6471	91	91	Jean-Baptiste GONNET	71.46	6360	89
15	Anthony WALL	70.42	6549	93	65	Rory SABBATINI	71.12	2987	42	93	Paul BROADHURST	71.47	6289	88
16	Peter HANSON	70.47	6765	96	66	Gonzalo FDEZ-CASTAÑO	71.14	6829	96	94	Robert ROCK	71.51	5935	83
16	Louis OOSTHUIZEN	70.47	6554	93	67	José Maria OLAZÁBAL	71.17	3274	46	95	Scott STRANGE	71.54	6081	85
18	Thongchai JAIDEE	70.48	7330	104	67	Keith HORNE	71.17	2135	30	95	Darren BECK	71.54	2003	28
18	Oliver WILSON	70.48	5920	84	69	Jyoti RANDHAWA	71.19	5553	78	97	Klas ERIKSSON	71.57	5296	74
20	Søren HANSEN	70.53	6771	96	69	Tim CLARK	71.19	2278	32	98	Alan MCLEAN	71.58	3221	45
20	David DRYSDALE	70.53	6841	97	71	Graeme STORM	71.21	7548	106	99	Steve WEBSTER	71.59	5942	83
22	Simon DYSON	70.55	7761	110	72	Stephen DODD	71.22	5840	82	99	Simon KHAN	71.59	6228	87
23	Justin ROSE	70.57	3246	46	73	Tano GOYA	71.26	5701	80	99	Nick DOUGHERTY	71.59	6515	91
24	Richard GREEN	70.59	4659	66	74	Markus BRIER	71.27	6129	86	99	Richie RAMSAY	71.59	6300	88
25	Bradley DREDGE	70.63	7063	100	75	Fabrizio ZANOTTI	71.29	5846	82					
25	Wen-chong LIANG	70.63	3037	43	75	Danny LEE	71.29	2709	38					
27	Ernie ELS	70.64	4097	58	77	Maarten LAFEBER	71.31	6632	93					
28	Robert-Jan DERKSEN	70.68	6008	85	78	Gary ORR	71.33	4779	67					
28	Danny WILLETT	70.68	6503	92										
30	Gareth MAYBIN	70.70	6929	98										
31	Søren KJELDSEN	70.71	6364	90										
31	Mardan MAMAT	70.71	1980	28										
33	Graeme MCDOWELL	70.73	5658	80										
33	Ross McGOWAN	70.73	6932	98										
35	Peter LAWRIE	70.77	6440	91										
35	Robert KARLSSON	70.77	2760	39										
37	Ignacio GARRIDO	70.79	6937	98										
37	Camilo VILLEGAS	70.79	2973	42										
39	David LYNN	70.80	6443	91										
39	Alvaro QUIROS	70.80	6089	86										
41	Jeev Milkha SINGH	70.81	4957	70										
42	Rodney PAMPLING	70.83	2975	42										
42	Luke DONALD	70.83	2975	42										
44	Raphaël JACQUELIN	70.85	7227	102										
45	Paul LAWRIE	70.87	5953	84										
46	Jamie DONALDSON	70.88	6875	97										
47	Ross FISHER	70.89	5317	75										
48	Adam SCOTT	70.90	2978	42										
49	Mark FOSTER	70.91	6666	94										
49	Tony CAROLAN	70.91	2411	34										

Rory McIlroy receives his Stroke Average award from Peter Barrett, Managing Director of Genworth Financial

Driving Distance (yds)

Pos	Name	Average Yards	Stats Rounds
1	**Alvaro QUIROS**	314.5	64
2	John DALY	307.9	24
3	Anton HAIG	304.3	61
4	Pelle EDBERG	303.3	93
5	Rory MCILROY	301.4	62
6	Daniel VANCSIK	301.1	83
7	Johan EDFORS	300.7	82
7	Bernd WIESBERGER	300.7	54
9	Lee WESTWOOD	299.8	66
10	Rafael CABRERA-BELLO	299.6	95
11	Alfredo GARCIA-HEREDIA	299.3	40
12	Danny WILLETT	299.1	84
13	Christian NILSSON	298.1	44
13	Ricardo GONZALEZ	298.1	71
15	Robert ROCK	297.7	78
16	Sergio GARCIA	297.6	36
17	Anthony SNOBECK	297.5	38
18	Alan MCLEAN	297.3	36
18	Thomas AIKEN	297.3	56
20	Wil BESSELING	296.9	68
21	Søren HANSEN	296.6	70
21	Paul WARING	296.6	63
23	Rafa ECHENIQUE	296.0	72
24	Åke NILSSON	295.9	56
25	Louis OOSTHUIZEN	295.8	76

Driving Accuracy (%)

Pos	Name	%	Stats Rounds
1	**Peter O'MALLEY**	79.5	54
2	Alessandro TADINI	74.6	81
3	John BICKERTON	74.3	64
4	Francesco MOLINARI	73.0	84
5	Peter LAWRIE	72.0	86
6	Anders HANSEN	70.8	72
7	Gary ORR	70.6	62
8	Ian POULTER	70.5	32
9	Richard STERNE	69.3	44
10	Ignacio GARRIDO	68.8	94
10	Graeme MCDOWELL	68.8	52
12	Steven O'HARA	68.6	60
13	Andrew COLTART	68.2	73
14	Seve BENSON	67.9	74
15	Richie RAMSAY	67.8	75
16	Felipe AGUILAR	67.7	78
16	Gareth MAYBIN	67.7	89
18	Stephen DODD	67.5	79
19	Stuart MANLEY	67.4	32
20	Fabrizio ZANOTTI	67.3	82
21	Anthony WALL	67.2	87
21	Marcus FRASER	67.2	78
23	Kenneth FERRIE	67.1	56
23	Scott STRANGE	67.1	76
25	Simon WAKEFIELD	66.8	82

Average Putts Per Round

Pos	Name	Putts per Round	Stats Rounds
1	**Thomas AIKEN**	28.3	56
2	Martin KAYMER	28.5	46
2	Michael LORENZO-VERA	28.5	76
4	Padraig HARRINGTON	28.7	28
4	Paul BROADHURST	28.7	80
6	Fredrik ANDERSSON HED	28.8	34
7	David HOWELL	28.9	68
7	Andrew MCLARDY	28.9	56
7	Patrik SJÖLAND	28.9	40
7	S S P CHOWRASIA	28.9	61
11	David FROST	29.0	51
11	Martin ERLANDSSON	29.0	73
11	John MELLOR	29.0	40
11	Simon DYSON	29.0	102
15	Damien MCGRANE	29.1	99
15	Søren KJELDSEN	29.1	67
15	Colin MONTGOMERIE	29.1	80
15	Robert KARLSSON	29.1	30
15	Pablo LARRAZÁBAL	29.1	92
15	Chapchai NIRAT	29.1	77
15	Tano GOYA	29.1	71
22	Richard GREEN	29.2	51
22	Henrik STENSON	29.2	46
22	Per-Ulrik JOHANSSON	29.2	36
22	Paul CASEY	29.2	25
22	Jeppe HULDAHL	29.2	78
22	Marcus FRASER	29.2	78
22	David HORSEY	29.2	82
22	Shiv KAPUR	29.2	80
22	Chinnarat PHADUNGSIL	29.2	38
31	Jeev Milkha SINGH	29.3	54
31	Marcus HIGLEY	29.3	46
31	Peter HANSON	29.3	75
31	Pelle EDBERG	29.3	93
31	Miguel Angel JIMÉNEZ	29.3	76
31	Stephen DODD	29.3	79
31	Michael CAMPBELL	29.3	34
31	Mikael LUNDBERG	29.3	73
31	John E MORGAN	29.3	41
31	Jamie DONALDSON	29.3	88
31	Louis OOSTHUIZEN	29.3	76
31	Branden GRACE	29.3	55

Greens In Regulation (%)

Pos	Name	%	Stats Rounds
1	**Sergio GARCIA**	79.8	36
2	Retief GOOSEN	78.5	32
3	Rory MCILROY	78.1	62
4	Søren HANSEN	77.4	70
4	Steven O'HARA	77.4	60
6	Ian POULTER	76.6	32
7	Alexander NOREN	76.2	78
8	Francesco MOLINARI	76.1	84
9	Stephen GALLACHER	75.9	36
10	Johan EDFORS	75.4	82
11	Ernie ELS	75.3	34
12	Justin ROSE	75.2	26
13	Ignacio GARRIDO	75.0	94
14	Lee WESTWOOD	74.8	66
15	Anthony WALL	74.7	87
15	Paul CASEY	74.7	25
17	Thomas LEVET	74.4	78
18	Oliver WILSON	74.0	58
19	Anders HANSEN	73.8	72
20	Charl SCHWARTZEL	73.3	74
21	Richard FINCH	72.9	72
22	Steve WEBSTER	72.8	71
23	Gareth MAYBIN	72.7	89
24	Thongchai JAIDEE	72.2	88
24	Ross FISHER	72.2	48

Sand Saves (%)

Pos	Name	%	Stats Rounds
1	**Robert KARLSSON**	74.3	30
2	Andrew MCLARDY	72.3	56
3	Francesco MOLINARI	70.8	84
4	Padraig HARRINGTON	68.8	28
5	Pablo LARRAZÁBAL	68.5	92
6	Richard BLAND	67.1	66
7	Rodney PAMPLING	66.7	24
7	David DIXON	66.7	74
9	Rory MCILROY	66.2	62
10	Alessandro TADINI	65.5	81
10	Thomas BJÖRN	65.5	62
12	Gonzalo FDEZ-CASTAÑO	64.6	80
12	Thomas AIKEN	64.6	56
14	Bradley DREDGE	64.0	95
15	Martin ERLANDSSON	63.9	73
15	Fredrik ANDERSSON HED	63.9	34
17	Alastair FORSYTH	63.2	66
18	Marc WARREN	63.0	74
19	Marcus HIGLEY	62.9	46
20	Marcel SIEM	62.8	87
21	Paul BROADHURST	62.7	80
22	Thongchai JAIDEE	62.6	88
23	Richard GREEN	62.5	51
23	Alexander NOREN	62.5	78
25	Iain PYMAN	62.2	33

Putts Per Green In Regulation

Pos	Name	Putts per GIR	Stats Rounds
1	**Thomas AIKEN**	1.717	56
2	Martin KAYMER	1.723	46
3	Paul CASEY	1.729	25
4	Charl SCHWARTZEL	1.739	74
5	Justin ROSE	1.741	26
5	Ian POULTER	1.741	32
7	Padraig HARRINGTON	1.743	28
7	Shiv KAPUR	1.743	80
9	Jeev Milkha SINGH	1.747	54
10	Lee WESTWOOD	1.748	66
10	Michael LORENZO-VERA	1.748	76
12	Sergio GARCIA	1.749	36
13	Miguel Angel JIMÉNEZ	1.751	76
14	David FROST	1.754	51
15	Tano GOYA	1.755	71
16	Andrew MCLARDY	1.757	56
17	Richard STERNE	1.758	44
18	Søren KJELDSEN	1.760	67
18	Marcus FRASER	1.760	78
20	Robert KARLSSON	1.761	30
20	Alvaro QUIROS	1.761	64
20	Rory MCILROY	1.761	62
23	Colin MONTGOMERIE	1.762	80
23	David DRYSDALE	1.762	86
23	Louis OOSTHUIZEN	1.762	76
23	Pablo LARRAZÁBAL	1.762	92
27	Peter LAWRIE	1.763	86
27	Paul BROADHURST	1.763	80
27	David HORSEY	1.763	82
30	Richard GREEN	1.764	51
31	Stephen DODD	1.765	79
32	Bradley DREDGE	1.766	95
32	Patrik SJÖLAND	1.766	40
34	Hennie OTTO	1.767	60
34	John E MORGAN	1.767	41
36	Francesco MOLINARI	1.768	84
37	Gareth MAYBIN	1.769	89
38	Brett RUMFORD	1.770	79
39	Maarten LAFEBER	1.771	86
39	Nick DOUGHERTY	1.771	76
39	Jeppe HULDAHL	1.771	78
39	S S P CHOWRASIA	1.771	61

Scrambles

Pos	Name	%	AVE SPR	AVE Missed GPR	Total Missed GIR	Total Scrambles	Stats Rounds
1	**Padraig HARRINGTON**	69.2	3.6	5	146	101	28
2	Martin KAYMER	67.8	3.4	5	233	158	46
3	Peter HANSON	64.3	3.3	5	389	250	75
4	Paul CASEY	63.2	2.9	5	114	72	25
5	Simon DYSON	63.1	3.7	6	591	373	102
6	Damien MCGRANE	62.8	3.6	6	573	360	99
7	Rodney PAMPLING	62.1	3.2	5	124	77	24
8	Robert-Jan DERKSEN	61.8	3.4	5	450	278	82
9	Søren KJELDSEN	61.7	3.4	6	371	229	67
10	Thongchai JAIDEE	61.6	3.1	5	440	271	88
11	Wen-chong LIANG	61.2	3.3	5	165	101	31
12	Robert KARLSSON	61.1	3.4	6	167	102	30
13	Anders HANSEN	60.5	2.8	5	339	205	72
13	Scott STRANGE	60.5	3.5	6	440	266	76
15	Richard GREEN	60.4	3.2	5	273	165	51
16	Henrik STENSON	60.3	3.6	6	272	164	46
16	Gonzalo FDEZ-CASTAÑO	60.3	3.5	6	459	277	80
18	Chapchai NIRAT	59.7	3.8	6	496	296	77
19	Jean-Baptiste GONNET	59.6	3.6	6	503	300	84
20	Miguel Angel JIMÉNEZ	59.5	3.1	5	395	235	76
21	Jamie DONALDSON	59.4	3.3	6	495	294	88
21	Louis OOSTHUIZEN	59.4	3.1	5	401	238	76
23	Francesco MOLINARI	59.1	2.5	4	362	214	84
24	Ernie ELS	58.9	2.6	4	151	89	34
24	David LYNN	58.9	3.2	6	479	282	87

THE 2009 EUROPEAN TOUR INTERNATIONAL SCHEDULE

DATE		EVENT	VENUE
2008			
Nov	6-9	**HSBC Champions**	Sheshan International GC, Shanghai, China
	20-23	**UBS Hong Kong Open**	Hong Kong GC, Fanling, Hong Kong
	27-30	**Sportsbet Australian Masters**	Huntingdale GC, Melbourne, Australia
Dec	11-14	**Alfred Dunhill Championship**	Leopard Creek CC, Mpumalanga, South Africa
	18-21	**South African Open Championship**	Pearl Valley Golf Estates, Paarl, Western Cape, South Africa
2009			
Jan	8-11	**Joburg Open**	Royal Johannesburg & Kensington GC, Johannesburg, South Africa
	9-11	***The Royal Trophy**	Amata Spring CC, Bangkok,Thailand
	15-18	**Abu Dhabi Golf Championship**	Abu Dhabi GC, Abu Dhabi, UAE
	22-25	**Commercialbank Qatar Masters presented by Dolphin Energy**	Doha GC, Doha, Qatar
	29-Feb 1	**Dubai Desert Classic**	Emirates GC, Dubai, UAE
Feb	12-15	**Maybank Malaysian Open**	Saujana G&CC, Kuala Lumpur, Malaysia
	19-22	**Johnnie Walker Classic**	The Vines Resort & CC, Perth, Australia
	26-1 Mar	**Enjoy Jakarta Indonesia Open**	New Kuta GC, Bali, Indonesia
	25-1 Mar	**WGC - Accenture Match Play**	Ritz-Carlton GC, Dove Mountain, Marana, Arizona, USA
Mar	12-15	**WGC - CA Championship**	Doral Golf Resort & Spa, Doral, Florida, USA
	19-22	**Madeira Islands Open BPI - Portugal**	Porto Santo Golfe, Madeira, Portugal
	26-29	**Open de Andalucia de Golf 09**	Real Club de Golf de Sevilla, Seville, Spain
Apr	2-5	**Estoril Open de Portugal**	Oitavos Dunes, Cascais, Portugal
	9-12	**MASTERS TOURNAMENT**	Augusta National GC, Georgia, USA
	16-19	**Volvo China Open**	Beijing CBD International GC, Beijing, China
	23-26	**Ballantine's Championship**	Pinx GC, Jeju Island, South Korea
	30-3 May	**Open de España**	PGA Golf de Catalunya, Girona, Spain
May	7-10	**BMW Italian Open**	Royal Park I Roveri, Turin, Italy
	14-17	**The 3 Irish Open**	County Louth GC, Baltray, Drogheda, Ireland
	21-24	**BMW PGA CHAMPIONSHIP**	Wentworth Club, Surrey, England
	28-31	**The European Open**	The London GC, Ash, Kent, England
Jun	4-7	**The Celtic Manor Wales Open**	The Celtic Manor Resort, City of Newport, Wales
	18-21	**SAINT-OMER OPEN presented by Neuflize OBC**	Aa Saint Omer GC, Lumbres, France
	18-21	**US OPEN CHAMPIONSHIP**	Bethpage State Park, Farmingdale, New York, USA
	25-28	**BMW International Open**	Golfclub München Eichenried, Munich, Germany
Jul	2-5	**Open de France ALSTOM**	Le Golf National, Paris, France
	9-12	**The Barclays Scottish Open**	Loch Lomond GC, Glasgow, Scotland
	16-19	**THE 138th OPEN CHAMPIONSHIP**	Ailsa Course, Turnberry, Ayrshire, Scotland
	23-26	**SAS Masters**	Barsebäck G&CC, Malmö, Sweden
	30-2 Aug	**Moravia Silesia Open presented by ALO Diamonds**	Prosper Golf Resort, Čeladná, Czech Republic
Aug	6-9	**WGC – Bridgestone Invitational**	Firestone CC, Akron, Ohio, USA
	13-16	**US PGA CHAMPIONSHIP**	Hazeltine National GC, Chaska, Minnesota, USA
	20-23	**KLM Open**	Kennemer G&CC, Zandvoort, The Netherlands
	27-30	**Johnnie Walker Championship at Gleneagles**	The Gleneagles Hotel, Perthshire, Scotland
Sept	3-6	**Omega European Masters**	Crans-sur-Sierre, Crans Montana, Switzerland
	10-13	**Mercedes-Benz Championship**	Golf Club Gut Lärchenhof, Cologne, Germany
	17-20	**Austrian Golf Open**	Fontana GC, Vienna, Austria
	24-27	*** The Vivendi Trophy with Seve Ballesteros**	Saint Nom-la-Bretèche, Paris, France
Oct	1-4	**Alfred Dunhill Links Championship**	Old Course, St Andrews, Carnoustie and Kingsbarns, Scotland
	8-11	**Madrid Masters**	Centro Nacional de Golf, Madrid, Spain
	15-18	**Portugal Masters**	Oceânico Victoria Golf Course, Vilamoura, Portugal
	22-25	**CASTELLÓ MASTERS Costa Azahar**	Club de Campo del Mediterráneo, Castellón, Spain
	29-1 Nov	**Barclays Singapore Open**	Sentosa GC, Singapore
	29-1 Nov	**Volvo World Match Play Championship**	Finca Cortesin GC, Casares, Spain
Nov	5-8	**WGC - HSBC Champions**	Sheshan International GC, Shanghai, China
	12-15	**UBS Hong Kong Open**	Hong Kong GC, Fanling, Hong Kong
	12-15	**JBWere Masters**	Kingston Heath GC, Melbourne, Australia
	19-22	**DUBAI WORLD CHAMPIONSHIP presented by: DP World**	Earth Course, Jumeirah Golf Estates, Dubai, UAE

WINNER	SCORE	FIRST PRIZE / PRIZE FUND
Sergio Garcia, ESP **	66-68-72-68=274 (-14)	€650,382 / €3,893,751
Wen-tang Lin, TPE **	65-69-64-67=265 (-15)	€327,383 / €1,996,575
Rod Pampling, AUS **	71-68-70-67=276 (-12)	€140,193 / €738,851
Richard Sterne, RSA	68-66-68-69=271 (-17)	€158,500 / €1,000,200
Richard Sterne, RSA **	72-69-67-66=274 (-14)	€158,500 / €1,007,670
Anders Hansen, DEN	71-68-64-66=269 (-15)	€174,350 / €1,121,436
Asia def Europe	10-6	€76,105 / €1,074,430***
Paul Casey, ENG	69-65-63-70=267 (-21)	€245,122 / €1,475,158
Alvaro Quiros, ESP	69-67-64-69=269 (-19)	€314,400 / €1,882,982
Rory McIlroy, NIR	64-68-67-70=269 (-19)	€323,514 / €1,930,002
Anthony Kang, USA	74-66-64-67=271 (-17)	€259,164 / €1,564,310
Danny Lee (AM), NZL	67-68-69-67=271 (-17)	€160,582^ / €1,412,780
Thongchai Jaidee, THA	71-69-67-69=276 (-12)	€163,867 / €981,417
Geoff Ogilvy, AUS	def Paul Casey ENG 4 and 3	€1,101,204 / €6,685,882
Phil Mickelson, USA	65-66-69-69=269 (-19)	€1,105,005 / €6,681,337
Tano Goya, ARG	68-68-69-73=278 (-6)	€116,660 / €704,182
Søren Kjeldsen, DEN	68-72-62-72=274 (-14)	€166,660 / €998,170
Michael Hoey, NIR**	66-76-69-66=277 (-7)	€208,330 / €1,261,205
Angel Cabrera, ARG**	68-68-69-71=276 (-12)	€1,005,748 / €5,647,429
Scott Strange, AUS	70-73-69-68=280 (-8)	€275,813 / €1,662,349
Thongchai Jaidee, THA**	66-71-77-70=284 (-4)	€350,000 / €2,112,582
Thomas Levet, FRA	64-67-71-68=270 (-18)	€333,330 / €2,000,000
Daniel Vancsik, ARG	68-65-69-65=267 (-17)	€216,660 / €1,297,620
Shane Lowry (AM), IRL**	67-62-71-71=271 (-17)	€500,000^/ €3,000,000
Paul Casey, ENG	69-67-67-68=271 (-17)	€750,000 / €4,553,916
Christian Cévaër, FRA	67-70-70-74=281 (-7)	€341,220 / €2,043,589
Jeppe Huldahl, DEN	69-71-68-67=275 (-9)	€343,086 / €2,073,926
Christian Nilsson, SWE	68-69-65-69=271 (-13)	€100,000 / €606,237
Lucas Glover, USA	69-64-70-73=276 (-4)	€952,152 / €5,288,326
Nick Dougherty, ENG	69-65-68-64=266 (-22)	€333,330 / €2,003,000
Martin Kaymer, GER**	62-72-69-68=271 (-13)	€666,660 / €4,047,916
Martin Kaymer, GER	69-65-66-69=269 (-15)	€597,339 / €3,512,475
Stewart Cink, USA**	66-72-71-69=278 (-2)	€866,557 / €4,857,633
Ricardo Gonzalez, ARG	68-68-77-69=282 (-10)	€166,660 / €1,011,916
Oskar Henningsson, SWE	70-71-67-67=275 (-13)	€330,330 / €2,003,000
Tiger Woods, USA	68-70-65-65=268 (-12)	€999,407 / €6,017,682
Y E Yang, KOR	73-70-67-70=280 (-8)	€942,125 / €5,223,214
Simon Dyson, ENG**	67-67-68-63=265 (-15)	€300,000 / €1,793,300
Peter Hedblom, SWE	72-68-68-67=275 (-13)	€269,895 / €1,603,154
Alexander Noren, SWE	65-70-63-66=264 (-20)	€333,330 / €1,996,350
James Kingston, RSA**	67-69-70-69=275 (-13)	€320,000 / €2,000,000
Rafael Cabrera-Bello, ESP	71-67-66-60=264 (-20)	€166,660 / €989,970
Great Britain & Ireland def Continental Europe	16½ - 11½	€65,000 / €1,150,000•
Simon Dyson, ENG	68-66-68-66=268 (-20)	€540,440 / €3,242,641
Ross McGowan, ENG	66-66-60-71=263 (-25)	€250,000 / €1,506,741
Lee Westwood, ENG	66-67-66-66=265 (-23)	€500,000 / €2,994,530
Michael Jonzon, SWE	64-68-65-67=264 (-20)	€333,330 / €2,029,865
Ian Poulter, ENG	66-64-72-72=274 (-10)	€554,127 / €3,318,713
Ross Fisher, ENG	def Anthony Kim, USA 4 and 3	€750,000 / €3,250,000+
Phil Mickelson, USA	69-66-67-69=271 (-17)	€807,575 / €4,694,030
Grégory Bourdy, FRA	64-67-63-67=261 (-19)	€279,288 / €1,658,956
Tiger Woods, USA	66-68-72-68=274 (-14)	€173,117 / €921,461
Lee Westwood, ENG	66-69-66-64=265 (-23)	€830,675 / €4,955,642

* - Denotes Approved Special Event
** - Denotes play-off
*** - Each member of the winning team received €76,105. Each member of the losing team received €38,052
• - Each member of the winning team received €65,000. Each member of the losing team received €50,000
^ - First prize allocated to second place
+ - Capped for The Race to Dubai €541,667 / €2,148,177

OMEGA MISSION HILLS WORLD CUP
Mission Hills Golf Club, China

L-R: Dr David Chu, Group Chairman, Mission Hills Group, Henrik Stenson, Robert Karlsson and Stephen Urquhart, President Omega

Global Progression

Japan: Ryuji Imada (left) and Toru Taniguchi

China: Zhang Lian-wei (left) and Liang Wen-chong

The growth and development of golf can be measured in many ways and unquestionably one event which has contributed to its global progression is the World Cup. Coincidentally, the rise and rise of Sweden as a powerful nation within the game has similarly demonstrated all that can be achieved within golf, so it was appropriate enough that for only the second time in their history Sweden should be the defending champions at the World Cup when it returned, in 2009, for a third successive time and a fourth time in total to the Mission Hills Golf Club in China.

Sweden won with Anders Forsbrand and Per-Ulrik Johansson in 1991 – five years after Ove Sellberg had become the first Swedish golfer to win on The European Tour – and in 2008 it was the turn of Robert Karlsson and Henrik Stenson. They won the Omega Mission Hills World Cup when, with a magnificent last round foursomes score of 63, they stormed from four shots behind Spain to move three shots clear with a 27 under par total of 261.

Karlsson declared: "This victory means a great deal for our country. The World Cup has always been a big event in Sweden. It's quite a new country for golf and to play for your country is great. If you look at the huge trophy you will see all the many impressive pairings that have won the World Cup. I hope that in time people might look back and say the same thing about us."

To many observers of this great game that would seem inevitable. Karlsson had already made history less than one month before arriving at Mission Hills by becoming the first Swedish golfer to win the Order of Merit - now The Race to Dubai - on The European Tour. Only a few months later it was the turn of Stenson to celebrate when he became only the third European golfer and the first from Sweden to win The Players Championship on the US PGA Tour. Stenson said: "It's a great honour to play for your country so we had a special week in China as we also won."

The World Cup has found a special home in China with the 55th edition in 2009 unfolding at Mission Hills where it was first played in 1995. It was inevitable, too, that the atmosphere would again be electric with that special flavour of tradition and expectation in the air. The trophy was first provided for competition in 1953 when John Jay Hopkins realised a dream to promote goodwill between nations through the Canada Cup. The increasing international image of the event was reflected by the name change in 1967 to the World Cup. The International Federation of PGA Tours became the custodians of the event in 2000. Omega and Mission Hills became partners in the World Cup in 2007.

South Africa: Rory Sabbatini (left) and Richard Sterne

Germany: Alex Cejka (left) and Martin Kaymer

England: Ross Fisher (left) and Ian Poulter

Ultimate Dream

THE EUROPEAN TOUR QUALIFYING SCHOOL
PGA Golf de Catalunya, Girona, Spain

L-R: Angel Gallardo, Vice-Chairman of the PGA European Tour Board of Directors, Oskar Henningsson and Qualifying School Director Mike Stewart

Chris Wood

When Sweden's Oskar Henningsson secured his maiden title on The European Tour International Schedule by capturing the Moravia Silesia Open presented by ALO Diamonds in August, he made two significant entries into golf's record books.

Not only did the 23 year old Swede become the 31st player to graduate from The European Tour Qualifying School – Final Stage and post a win the following season, he also, and perhaps more impressively, became only the third player in history – following Gordon Brand Jnr and José Maria Olazábal – to triumph the following season having won the Qualifying School itself.

Henningsson carded five sub 70 rounds out of six including a three under par closing 69 for a 21 under par total of 409 to win by four shots from Australian Wayne Ormsby and local favourite Carlos Del Moral at PGA Golf de Catalunya near Girona.

It was one of several fine performances, another of note coming from Northern Irishman Michael Hoey whose final round five under par 67 was the best score of the day and one which helped the 29 year old climb to eighth place overall among the 32 qualifiers. Hoey, of course, became the 30th graduate to win the following season when he captured the Estoril Open de Portugal in April.

The 2008 Qualifying School – Final Stage once again produced drama and tension, elation and exasperation, with the ultimate dream of Membership of The European Tour at stake.

The long and winding road that led to PGA Golf de Catalunya, to where the School returned in 2009, was perfectly illustrated by the progress of Danny Willett in 2008. The son of a preacher from Sheffield – who won the English Amateur Championship in 2007, played in the Walker Cup that year and became Number One Amateur in the World – won Stage One (Section A) at Fleesensee Golf and Country Club in Germany, then came through Stage Two at Sherry Golf Jerez in Spain before finishing fourth at PGA Golf de Catalunya.

Furthermore the quality of the field for the Final Stage was reflected by the presence of European Tour winners Andrew Coltart, Joakim Haeggman and Santiago Luna – all of whom finished in the leading 32 – as did Chris Wood. In The 2008 Open Championship at Royal Birkdale, Wood, then an amateur, finished fifth behind Padraig Harrington and, coincidentally, he finished in the same position at the School. The Englishman continued his Open odyssey in 2009 when, this time as a professional, he finished tied third with Lee Westwood at Turnberry.

PGA Golf de Catalunya is situated in the north east of Spain in the town of Caldas between Barcelona and Girona. It is the 14th venue in total to stage the event and features two courses – the Green Course and the Red Course – both of which were designed by two of the most renowned figures in European golf, England's Neil Coles MBE and Angel Gallardo of Spain.

The club is no stranger to hosting top level competition – Thomas Björn won the 1999 Gene Sarazen World Open there; Brian Davis the 2000 Peugeot Open de España; and Jerry Bruner the 2001 European Seniors Tour Championship. Mike Stewart, the Qualifying School Director, said: "It presents an excellent challenge for the players striving to gain that highly regarded Membership status."

Danny Willett

Michael Hoey

Sir Terry Matthews –
Fulfilment of a Vision

October 1, 2010 will mark the realisation of a dream for Sir Terry Matthews when The Ryder Cup takes place in Wales for the first time at his impressive Celtic Manor Resort. Or perhaps the fulfilment of a vision is a more appropriate description for the achievement of a highly successful businessman who is not given to flights of fancy.

What started, back in 1980, as a modest investment for Wales' first billionaire in creating the original 17-bedroom Celtic Manor Hotel on the very site where he himself had been born, became a bold ambition to stage the greatest team tournament in golf and one of the world's most captivating sporting spectacles.

The razzmatazz of The Ryder Cup was certainly a long way off when Sir Terry noticed a boarded-up old mansion for sale on a trip home to South Wales from Canada, where he had made his fortune as a telecommunications entrepreneur. This was not just the area where he grew up, this was the very building where he had been brought into the world during its former life as the Lydia Beynon Maternity Hospital.

Sir Terry's decision to buy his birthplace was not, however, born purely of sentiment. Disappointed by the lack of local hotel accommodation for Canadian engineers and managers who were helping set up a new European manufacturing and office base for his Mitel company at nearby Caldicot, he realised that here stood an estate which enjoyed fantastic access adjacent to the M4 motorway yet it was situated among acres of rolling parkland and wooded hills. Here was a position worthy of a top-class business and leisure resort.

Without the time to play himself, Sir Terry's interest in golf was fired initially by its commercial appeal. He saw golf as the sport played by business people and the golf course as the place where business deals were struck.

A chance meeting with a legendary golf course architect turned a vague notion of wanting to add a golf course to his new hotel into a reality and led eventually to ambitions to stage The Ryder Cup. Enjoying lunch in a Floridian golf clubhouse at Fort Lauderdale, Sir

Terry became increasingly curious when he heard a diner at a neighbouring table being addressed as Mr Jones.

When asked about any Welsh ancestry, the man introduced himself as Robert Trent Jones and explained his family had hailed from Aberystwyth before emigrating to the United States when he was a small boy. It was not long before Sir Terry had persuaded Trent Jones to make the trip to Wales and take a look at the land he had earmarked for a golf course at Celtic Manor.

There was one nervy moment during the first visit when Sir Terry inadvertently drove Trent Jones into a marsh and the pair ended up having to abandon their Land Rover, knee-deep in water, to continue the trek on foot. But Trent Jones, then in his 80s, took the adventure in his stride and was soon persuaded to design his first course in the land of his fathers - the original Roman Road course at The Celtic Manor Resort.

Another man persuaded to share Sir Terry's vision was Jim McKenzie who left behind the head greenkeeper's job at the

West Course at Wentworth Club to oversee construction of the Roman Road course and its preparation for play. The course opened in 1995 but there was little time to admire the view from the vast, timber-beamed Lodge Clubhouse as expansion at Celtic Manor continued apace.

Just four years later, a second championship course, Wentwood Hills, was added along with the massive Resort Hotel, a £120 million, 330-bedroom extension onto the existing Celtic Manor Hotel which itself had grown from 17 to 70 bedrooms between 1982 and 1999.

With luxury spa and huge convention centre, the Resort Hotel was immediately bestowed five-star status and Wentwood Hills was accorded similar rave reviews when present and future Ryder Cup captains, Mark James and Ian Woosnam, played an exhibition match to mark its official opening in front of huge galleries.

Plummeting 100 metres downhill on the second and third holes, the course offered some great views and spectacular challenges when it hosted The Celtic Manor Wales Open from 2000-2004 but

Colin Montgomerie and Corey Pavin

Above Captains Colin Montgomerie and Corey Pavin are interviewed by Chris Evans at The 'Year to Go' Gala Dinner at The Celtic Manor Resort

Bryn Terfel and John Owen-Jones

Chris Evans and Sir Terry Matthews

George O'Grady, Chief Executive of The European Tour

Rt Hon Rhodri Morgan, First Minister for Wales

the climb back over the closing holes was unpopular with some players. More seriously, as Ryder Cup ambitions crystallised into a formal bid with Wales in 2000, the hillside included a couple of ravines and guaranteeing the movement and safety of tens of thousands spectators through these sections was going to present obstacles.

At this point, having acquired new land alongside the lower section of the course, Sir Terry made one more bold and determined gesture by agreeing to build nine new holes to combine with the nine, existing flatter holes of Wentwood Hills and create The Twenty Ten Course, purpose-built for staging The Ryder Cup.

His energy and commitment was sufficient for tournament organisers to take him at his word and, for the first time, to award a Ryder Cup 'off-plan' to a course not yet laid out. In September 2001, the historic decision was announced to award Wales its first Ryder Cup to take place at The Celtic Manor Resort in 2010.

Building nine holes from scratch has allowed course architect Ross McMurray, of European Golf Design, and the team at Celtic Manor to factor in not just a number of golf holes designed specifically for the drama of team match play golf, but also to consider the needs of the spectators from the outset.

With 45,000 spectators expected every day, and only four matches out on the course at any one time during the first two days, it was of paramount

The Celtic Manor Resort

importance to offer ticket-holders the best possible view of the action. The Twenty Ten Course does just this by turning the steep hillside, the old disadvantage of Wentwood Hills, into a huge advantage as it now flanks the closing holes, allowing spectators a great view over not only the decisive action at the end of a match but also many more holes in the valley floor below.

A second large and luxurious clubhouse, built to serve The Twenty Ten Course, commands one of these vantage points and overlooking the 18th green is a full-length balcony where no doubt the winning champagne will be uncorked as soon as the final putt has dropped on Sunday evening. Inside are sumptuous locker rooms, bars, a restaurant and a private members lounge with leather chesterfields and high-

The Twenty Ten clubhouse

backed armchairs evoking the traditional elegance of the gentlemen's club.

Costing £16 million, construction of the new course and clubhouse was not without its challenges in a Site of Special Scientific Interest. Wildlife habitats, most notably those of otters and dormice, had to be preserved and archaeology teams accommodated as more and more Roman remains were discovered. Merely a couple of miles from the old Roman fort of Isca, now the town of Caerleon, several important discoveries were made including a soldier's grave, pottery kilns and villa foundations.

Caerleon is still home to Britain's best-preserved Roman amphitheatre, a closely mown central stage surrounded by grassy terraces. Two thousand years later, a new amphitheatre has taken shape. The Twenty Ten awaits... bring on the gladiators.

Paul Williams
The Celtic Manor Resort

L-R: Chris Evans, Colin Montgomerie, Gareth Edwards, Corey Pavin and Bryn Terfel

keeping **The European Tour** on course

Card of The Twenty Ten Course

Hole	Yds	Mtrs	Par
1	465	425	4
2	610	558	5
3	189	173	3
4	461	422	4
5	433	396	4
6	422	386	4
7	213	195	3
8	439	401	4
9	580	530	5
Out	**3812**	**3486**	**36**
10	210	192	3
11	562	514	5
12	458	419	4
13	189	173	3
14	485	443	4
15	377	345	4
16	499	456	4
17	211	193	3
18	575	526	5
In	**3566**	**3261**	**35**
Total	**7378**	**6747**	**71**

Ryder Cup Results: 1979-2008

1979 The Greenbrier, White Sulphur Springs, West Virginia, USA
Europe: 11 –USA 17

1981 Walton Heath, Surrey, England
Europe 9½ - USA 18½

1983 PGA National Golf Club, Palm Beach Gardens, Florida, USA
Europe 13½ - USA 14½

1985 The Belfry, Sutton Coldfield, West Midlands, England
Europe 16½ - USA 11½

1987 Muirfield Village, Columbus, Ohio, USA
Europe 15 - USA 13

1989 The Belfry, Sutton Coldfield, West Midlands, England
Europe 14 - USA 14 (Europe retained Cup)

1991 Ocean Course, Kiawah Island, South Carolina, USA
Europe 13½ - USA 14½

1993 The Belfry, Sutton Coldfield, West Midlands, England
Europe 13 - USA 15

1995 Oak Hill Country Club, Rochester, New York, USA
Europe 14½ - USA 13½

1997 Club de Golf Valderrama, Sotogrande, Spain
Europe 14½ - USA 13½

1999 The Country Club, Brookline, Massachusetts, USA
Europe 13½ - USA 14½

2002 The Belfry, Sutton Coldfield, West Midlands, England
Europe 15½ - USA 12½

2004 Oakland Hills Country Club, Bloomfield Township, Michigan, USA
Europe 18½ - USA 9½

2006 The K Club, Straffan, Co. Kildare, Ireland
Europe 18½ - USA 9½

2008 Valhalla Golf Club, Louisville, Kentucky, USA
Europe 11½ - USA 16½

Ryder Cup - Future Venues

2010	The Celtic Manor Resort, City of Newport, Wales
2012	Medinah Country Club, Medinah, Illinois, USA
2014	The Gleneagles Hotel, Perthshire, Scotland
2016	Hazeltine National Golf Club, Chaska, Minnesota, USA
2018	TBC
2020	Whistling Straits, Kohler, Wisconsin, USA

Colin Montgomerie's Hole by Hole Guide to The Twenty Ten Course

I was delighted and honoured, for many reasons, to be given the opportunity to captain The European Team for The 2010 Ryder Cup as the competition has been such a huge part of my life. What is also very special is that this will be the first Ryder Cup to be played on a course built specifically to host the match. It is set up to challenge the best and, being a course with a whole host of tempting options and punishing hazards, there will be drama every step of the way. It is going to be an extraordinary week for everyone especially, of course, Sir Terry Matthews, the visionary behind not only Wales' Ryder Cup bid, but also the development and continued success of The Celtic Manor Resort itself.

Can you enjoy a Ryder Cup course? You don't really have time to enjoy each hole but what you do enjoy is the competition and the competitive element of trying to beat the man across the fairway from you. You just want your particular game to be finished as early as possible. The nerves, very apparent on the first, might fade a little on the front nine but they will begin to kick in again from the 12th onwards because from there, every shot is key. From there, it really matters. From there it comes down to which player can handle what is put in front of him. That is what The Ryder Cup is all about – there is nothing like it.

Hole 1 - Par 4 - 465 yards; 425 metres

This is a very challenging opening hole. Go left and a cluster of deep bunkers at the elbow of the left hand dog-leg threaten to swallow the ball, but the angle of the green is in your favour coming in from this side. Go right, play safe, and you face a tougher approach with the entry to the green guarded by another two bunkers. Also to the right of the green is a swale which the ball can run down ten to 12 paces and well below the putting surface, plus there is another steep swale at the back which will take anything big. But, in all honesty, you can forget trying to analyse too much what you want to do or need to do on the first hole of a Ryder Cup because it is simply all about pressure. If you can find the fairway then fantastic as that will give you some semblance of order and a chance to hit the green. A par is a great score on the first hole of a Ryder Cup. Under the scrutiny of a home crowd, and following on from the three days of build up in the week itself, that first tee shot is the most pressure a lot of players will ever feel. On that first morning it builds and builds from the range to the putting green and then with that walk from the putting green to the first tee itself. The eyes of the world are on you. I'll be there as will Corey for his Team but ultimately it is down to the player to compose himself and hit the shot. That's why I say par is a great score. Trust me.

Hole 2 - Par 5 – 610 yards; 558 metres

Once you have got the pressure and tension of the first hole of your Ryder Cup match out of the way, I really believe this is the hole where you will see the first birdies of The 2010 Ryder Cup. I know it might not mean much in the overall outcome of the match as it comes so early but, if you can get a birdie, it will help you settle. This is a good hole, played alongside the River Usk. The drive demands accuracy with a narrow fairway that looks like a ribbon featuring deep bunkers on both sides. Even for the long hitters this is a tough hole to get up in two. Anything a tad off-line to the left will be swept away by the contours of the green and if you go down the swale to the right you can be 15 paces away, six feet below the green and facing a devilish shot. So all things being equal you are more likely to make an up and down birdie than a two putt birdie. There were only two eagles here in The 2009 Celtic Manor Wales Open, but 80 birdies.

Hole 2

Hole 3

Hole 3 – Par 3 – 189 yards; 173 metres

Because of the shape of the green on the first of the par threes, the pin placement is crucial here. There is a run off at the back and short is the water. Left is the plateau but if they put the pin half up on the right it is not easy there either. Because pin placement is crucial, it means that club selection becomes vital with the carry over water to deal with first. I will be on this tee with my players to give some advice if they feel they need me to. If you have managed to settle down on the second hole and hopefully have made a birdie four, then you are into the round and the match. There are no excuses now. I can understand the first and second causing a flutter or two, because it's The Ryder Cup, but you are now on your way.

Hole 4 – Par 4 – 461 yards; 422 metres

This is a hole which lends itself to a great second shot because the correct distance will be rewarded. It is a relatively simple drive, often into the prevailing wind, but nevertheless you still have to hit it authoritatively with two strategically placed bunkers to deal with. A lot of the new holes on The Twenty Ten Course have been designed with the distance control of the second shot in mind so the key here is most probably the approach. The biggest danger is the contouring of the green – it's not too difficult for the ball to fall off the putting surface – so the key is to make sure your ball is up so quite often it can be one more club that you think.

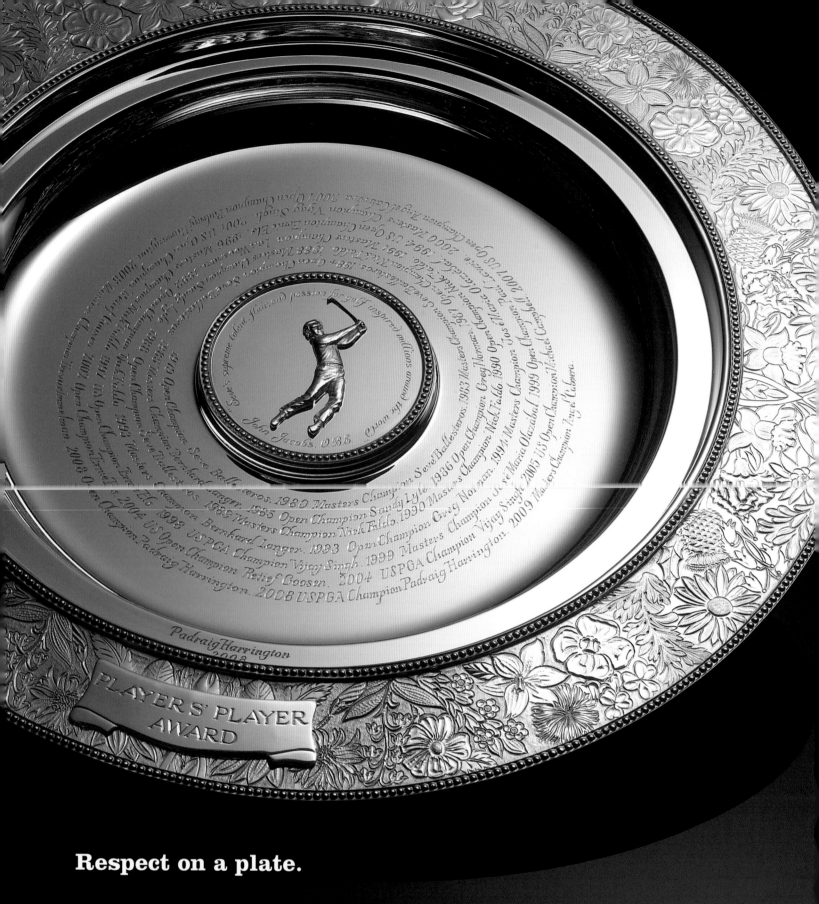

Respect on a plate.

THOMAS LYTE

Awarded to the golfer who has earned the respect of his peers,
The Players' Player Award took over 250 hours to handcraft
from sterling silver and gold by the Thomas Lyte silversmiths.

The complete Thomas Lyte collection, including luxury
leather accessories, silver vault and the bespoke service,
can be found online at thomaslyte.com.

Hole 5 – Par 4 – 433 yards; 396 metres

Another very good hole with the prevailing wind now behind you and again the second shot is crucial here. Short is no good because you roll down the bank into the water and big is perhaps worse in some ways because it is very difficult to get up and down from that side. So shot control is vital which means you have to be in the fairway. If you are not in the fairway, you are not hitting the green and especially in October when the grass in the rough will probably be wet and long. So you must hit the fairway which is no easy task. A little wayward and you could be snared by one of several bunkers. This will be an exciting time, too, because in the Friday and Saturday sessions, all the matches will be on the course by now, all the TVs will be up and running as will all the scoreboards. You can't really miss the scoreboards on the golf course as they are massive and they are on every hole. I actually think it is important to look at the scores to see how the contest is progressing and especially important if the scoreboard is all blue which we hope it will be. My earpiece will be blazing away with information from my Assistant Captains with each of the four matches. This is what The Ryder Cup is all about. Fantastic!

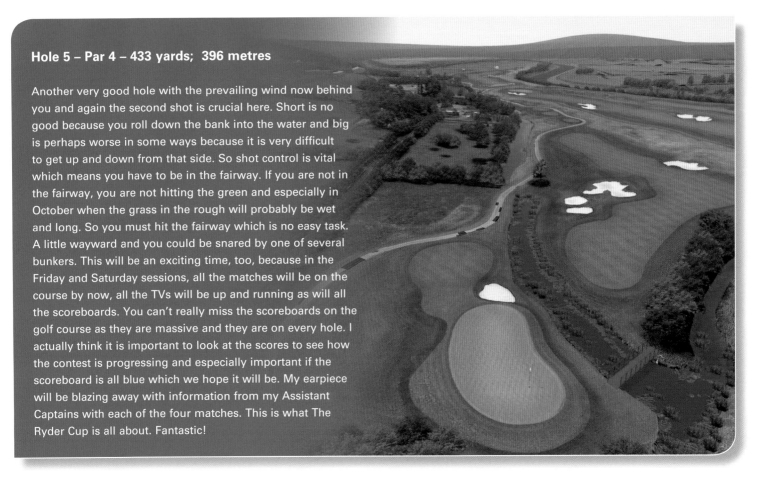

Hole 6 – Par 4 – 422 yards; 386 metres

The first of the remodelled holes. It is a good hole with water on the right which can heighten anxiety for the tee shot if you happen to leak one off to the right. Again the second shot is vital. The two bunkers left and front of the green offer protection, another deepened bunker at the back is a further threat but the hole is at its most demanding when the pin is on the right hand side of the green. Judge your approach wrongly, and the ball will trickle away into a watery grave.

Hole 7

Hole 6

Hole 7 – Par 3 – 213 yards; 195 metres

I think this is a great hole. Again, it depends on what is happening elsewhere but I will probably be on the tee once again here with my players if they want me to be. I don't want to confuse the issue but I want to help if possible. Remember I am the only person who can give advice to the players. If there is something one of my assistants wants to say to a player, he has to radio me and I can go and talk to that player. Actually the par threes are very well spaced out on The Twenty Ten Course because after this it is the tenth, the 13th and the 17th so, if I have to, I can actually get round to all of those tees with all of the matches. The advice here is straightforward – miss the large bunker that runs the length of the green on the left and the deep one to the right.....and get the ball close to the pin!

Hole 8 – Par 4 – 439 yards; 401 metres

A tough hole, with fairway bunkers left and right, and I have made it even tougher. I spoke with Jim McKenzie, the Director of Golf Courses and Estates at The Celtic Manor Resort, and asked that his team introduce a run-off to the right of the green. I want the pin on the right hand side here, and this will cause problems. It's a good hole and in truth your drive should find the straight and narrow. So again the second shot will be the key with greenside bunkers to the front and rear of the green as well as 'Monty's Incline' to now deal with. It takes you only six or seven paces away but it will be well below the green, so it really is a delicate one back.

Hole 8

Hole 9 – Par 5 – 580 yards; 530 metres

If you need a psychological boost then there is nothing quite like winning the ninth and heading for the inward half – rather like scoring in the last minute before half-time. It will be an exciting hole, too, as we will be playing each day from the forward tee so the green is reachable in two. You're going to see a number of birdies – especially in the fourballs. Nevertheless you must be careful with the drive to avoid two menacing bunkers to the right. If you pass the first test then the next one is to find the sanctuary of the green and most importantly avoid the huge bunker front right which quite recently received a facelift and the very deep pot bunker on the left. If the pin is back left and you go in that pot bunker, you will not see the bottom of the flag. By the way there is 2,500 tons of sand in the bunkers on The Twenty Ten and at £30 a ton that provides a good indication of what it costs to build a well protected, great course.

Hole 10 – Par 3 – 210 yards; 192 metres

The pin position on this hole is vital. The green slopes not just from back to front but it also slopes right to left so you have to hit that half of the green to give yourself any sort of putt at all. I will be there again because the wind swirls around at this hole. What you feel on the tee is not necessarily what is happening at the green so I'll definitely be there to offer advice. Selecting the right club is paramount because the green is surrounded by bunkers – two deep ones front left, a deep pot bunker tight to the green on the right and another one at the back which really comes into play when the pin is at the rear of the green. By the way, this was the 12th on the old Wentwood Hills course and where Paul McGinley beat Paul Lawrie and Daren Lee in a play-off for The 2001 Celtic Manor Wales Open.

Hole 10

Hole 12

Hole 12 – Par 4 – 458 yards; 419 metres

We are now coming to a great series of holes. These next three holes are excellent and will be right in the heart of each and every match. The second shot here plays uphill so there can be the tendency for the approach shots to come up short if you are not careful especially, once again, in October. Because it will be a little colder and because we are down in a valley at sea level, the ball will not fly as far. I'll be telling my players to be careful here because when I have played The Celtic Manor Wales Open, my second shot has come up short on numerous occasions and the lake that borders the front of the green is ready and waiting to swallow the ball.

Hole 11 – Par 5 – 562 yards; 514 metres

This is the big eagle chance on the golf course. There were eight here in The 2009 Celtic Manor Wales Open and expect to see more – hopefully from Europe – in Ryder Cup week. This is a good hole providing you hit the twisting, narrow fairway. That means missing the water to the left and a raised bunker to the right. If you do that, you can reach the green and you can do that in two on this hole because it is also largely downhill. There is a big swale to the left of the green - behind a deep, cavernous bunker which has been rebuilt – but you would be unlucky to go in the water. Two other slightly smaller, though still quite deep, bunkers help to guard the green but the spectators will see plenty of spectacular shots to the putting surface with the chance of setting up an eagle putt.

Hole 13 – Par 3 – 189 yards; 173 metres

This is a very good, very dangerous par three. The tee shot is over water so short is not great but distance control is vital because the two bunkers to the back left of the putting surface have been redesigned to be deeper and more of a hazard. So by all means take enough club to clear the water but be careful to stop short of the bunkers. If you are in a bunker at the back then the recovery shot from there must be played with precision – if the ball comes out a shade too quickly then it can gather pace across a fast green and disappear into the water.

Hole 14 – Par 4 – 485 yards; 443 metres

This, in my opinion, is the best hole on the golf course which is borne out by the fact that it was ranked the toughest at The 2009 Celtic Manor Wales Open. It demands a great drive followed by a fantastic second shot which comes in at an angle now. We used to be able to drive over the water, a carry of some 265 yards but because the new tee is further back, you can't do that now so you have to aim your tee shot left which leaves a demanding second shot in at an angle. Much depends, of course, from where the wind is blowing – if it's the prevailing wind then it will be behind the players sweeping straight up the valley from Bristol towards Monmouth. It could be a driver, four iron type of hole in October, and the atmosphere will be terrific with thousands of spectators on the embankment that surrounds the rear of the green. In some ways the 12th, 13th and 14th holes are the crux of the golf course - the Amen Corner of The Twenty Ten Course if you like - key holes and vital holes in match play not least for the fact that there are not many holes left if you get into trouble round there. You can be one down going to the 12th tee and quite comfortably two up when you stand on the 15th tee.

Hole 15

Hole 15 – Par 4 – 377 yards; 345 metres

The 14th might be the best hole on the golf course but I think the 15th is the best match play hole thanks largely to the fact that it is driveable and everybody will be going for it. From the elevated tee you can now see the green but you need to fire the ball over the ridge of trees to a putting surface that sits high and facing you. I'm pretty sure that no-one will go left now, and so the fairway has been rendered obsolete. However, if you do stray left of the green you are down into the creek and if you go right you are left with an almost impossible chip and putt. The green is also guarded by two bunkers; the one on the left is big and deep so if you are in there you will not see the pin. If the pin is back right, then from that bunker it's a good 30 yard shot. So, yes, great excitement and viewing for the crowds, especially with the amphitheatre-like effect that the hole naturally creates, but plenty for the players to consider with the business end of the match approaching.

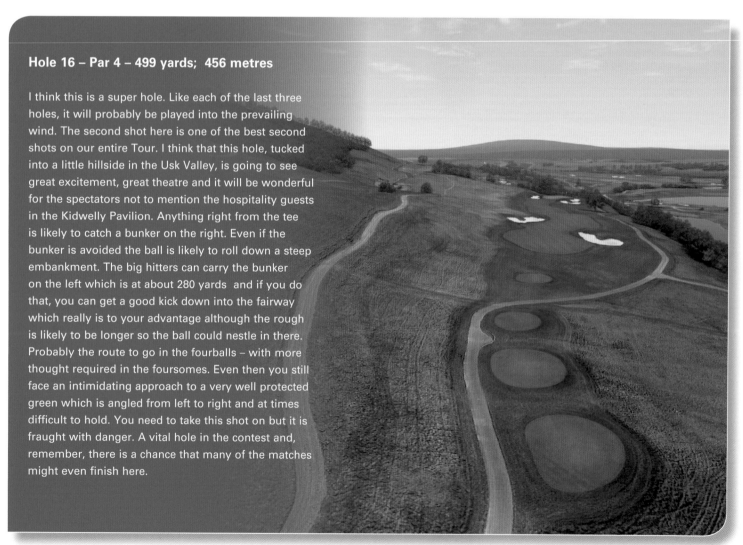

Hole 16 – Par 4 – 499 yards; 456 metres

I think this is a super hole. Like each of the last three holes, it will probably be played into the prevailing wind. The second shot here is one of the best second shots on our entire Tour. I think that this hole, tucked into a little hillside in the Usk Valley, is going to see great excitement, great theatre and it will be wonderful for the spectators not to mention the hospitality guests in the Kidwelly Pavilion. Anything right from the tee is likely to catch a bunker on the right. Even if the bunker is avoided the ball is likely to roll down a steep embankment. The big hitters can carry the bunker on the left which is at about 280 yards and if you do that, you can get a good kick down into the fairway which really is to your advantage although the rough is likely to be longer so the ball could nestle in there. Probably the route to go in the fourballs – with more thought required in the foursomes. Even then you still face an intimidating approach to a very well protected green which is angled from left to right and at times difficult to hold. You need to take this shot on but it is fraught with danger. A vital hole in the contest and, remember, there is a chance that many of the matches might even finish here.

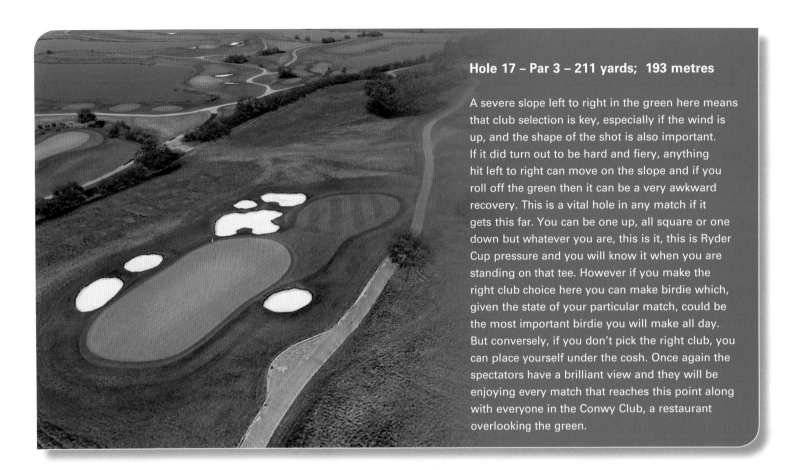

Hole 17 – Par 3 – 211 yards; 193 metres

A severe slope left to right in the green here means that club selection is key, especially if the wind is up, and the shape of the shot is also important. If it did turn out to be hard and fiery, anything hit left to right can move on the slope and if you roll off the green then it can be a very awkward recovery. This is a vital hole in any match if it gets this far. You can be one up, all square or one down but whatever you are, this is it, this is Ryder Cup pressure and you will know it when you are standing on that tee. However if you make the right club choice here you can make birdie which, given the state of your particular match, could be the most important birdie you will make all day. But conversely, if you don't pick the right club, you can place yourself under the cosh. Once again the spectators have a brilliant view and they will be enjoying every match that reaches this point along with everyone in the Conwy Club, a restaurant overlooking the green.

Hole 18 – Par 5 – 575 yards; 526 metres

If you have got this far in your match, the tension will be palpable. The forward tee is being used for The 2010 Ryder Cup, making the green reachable in two and presents possible eagle opportunities - for my Team, hopefully! I think it plays a much better two shot par five than it does a three shot par five so I wanted to be able to have the chance to go for the green, which is protected by two astonishingly good bunkers, over the water in two. I think that plays to our advantage as I do believe that, as a Tour, we hit the ball longer than the Americans do and I want to use that and the home course advantage as much as possible. If you are in the bunker on the left and the pin is at the front of the green then it is a tricky recovery as it is not impossible for the ball to trickle down into the water. The atmosphere will be incredible, too, as you are playing into that big natural amphitheatre of spectators which will be packed to the rafters every day. Trust me, if you have won your match, the walk up that hill from the 18th green to the clubhouse will be nothing. You'll float up the hill with a point in your bag. If you've lost, though, it'll be a mountain.

> PinPoint
> VISUALISATION
> Graphics courtesy of PinPoint Visualisation Limited

Hole 18

Colin Montgomerie –
The 2010 European Ryder Cup Captain

Colin Montgomerie has thrived in many arenas during a glittering career of record breaking individual success. Yet, it is his achievement in a team event which unquestionably best defines the passion and pride of this unique sporting figure.

Representing Europe in eight Ryder Cup matches, he was never beaten in a singles contest, but his influence in a period of unprecedented European success runs much deeper than that.

Montgomerie has been the catalyst, the leader and the closer. He is the most talked about European golfer of his generation and even though, in The Ryder Cup, he was only ever one individual of a dedicated dozen, he would invariably come to the fore.

Perhaps this was best illustrated in the 2004 contest at Oakland Hills where the talismanic Scot had been the grateful recipient of a wildcard selection. Captain Bernhard Langer did not dare take on the Americans in their own backyard without him.

Montgomerie started and finished the job. Partnering Padraig Harrington to a 2 and 1 victory in the opening match against the American 'dream-team' of Phil Mickelson and Tiger Woods, he helped set the tone for a stunning three days in Detroit. When he then holed the winning putt on the final green in Sunday's singles to edge out the doughty David Toms, Montgomerie ensured the trophy would remain in European hands.

It was little wonder that, during the press conference which followed the 18 ½ - 9 ½ victory, Langer's Team rose as one to applaud the man who had long since been Europe's rock. His eleven peers, players he had often beaten over the years on The European Tour, were determined to show the world precisely what he meant to his continent.

Born in Glasgow in June 1963, Colin Stuart Montgomerie OBE grew into a colossus of the European game with 31 Tour victories to his name. All that has ever been missing is a Major title. Twice he has lost play-offs, in the 1994 US Open Championship and in the US PGA Championship the following year. He has been runner up in two more US Opens and in The Open Championship at St Andrews in 2005, the year he claimed his record eighth Harry Vardon Trophy as European Number One.

They say golfing greatness is defined by the Majors, but Montgomerie is perhaps the exception to that rule. Despite winning all of The European Tour's biggest prizes, The Ryder Cup – where he has starred in a record equalling five victories – provides the Scot with his greatness.

No-one who was there will ever forget the way he held his nerve at Club de Golf Valderrama in 1997 to secure a half point and the overall victory for Europe in a tense singles decider against Scott Hoch. He also revelled in the responsibility of being sent out first in the singles matches by skipper Sam Torrance at The Belfry in 2002, once again coming up against that man Hoch, but this time trouncing him 5 and 4.

Crucially, he did the same job to similar effect for Ian Woosnam at The K Club in 2006 where once again David Toms was his victim on the final green.

Now it is Montgomerie's turn to decide the batting order. The European Tour's Tournament Committee jumped at the chance of appointing him Captain as soon as he made it clear he would be up for the job at The Celtic Manor Resort. He will lead Europe with the passion that has been the hallmark of his Ryder Cup career.

Pride of place in his Perthshire home is a unique plinth that displays the eight Harry Vardon Trophies he has amassed since 1993. Victory in Wales might just prompt an alteration, with space being made for a replica of Samuel Ryder's famous golden chalice, a trophy that, in so many ways, defines this extraordinary golfing figure.

Iain Carter
BBC Radio Five Live

6, 7, 5, 6, 7, 7, 9, 7, 5, 6, 6, 7, 8, 6, 7, 6, 8, 5, but happy.

We all get those days.
Where you seriously consider
packing it all in and taking up
darts or something.
But even a bad round here
has its positives.
Stunning championship courses.
Very reasonable green fees.
No pretentious nonsense.
A good walk through our
beautiful countryside.
And best of all, in Wales
tomorrow's always another day.

Wales: Host Nation for
The 2010 Ryder Cup

golfasitshouldbe.com

RYDER CUP 2010
Wales
Cymru

Wales
Cymru

Corey Pavin –
The 2010 United States Ryder Cup Captain

They call him 'The Bulldog' and Corey Pavin, the United States Ryder Cup Captain for 2010 is, like his sobriquet, fiercely loyal and patriotic to the core. He firmly believes his body is filled with the spirit and tradition of the contest and all it means to his fellow countrymen. "The Ryder Cup is in my blood," he said. "If you cut my arm open, Ryder Cup would just pour out."

Some quote. What is more, he is deadly serious. From the day, in 1991, when he urged on the American galleries at Kiawah Island in his famous camouflage cap in support of the troops engaged in Desert Storm, the biennial gathering has not just trickled through his veins – it has surged.

One thing is certain then, Colin Montgomerie and his European Team will have the toughest of opponents at the helm at The Celtic Manor Resort in October 2010.

Normal professional golfers enjoy team golf but put their true heart and soul into the individual game. Not so Pavin. Skippering the US Team has been his prime ambition since his Kiawah Island debut. "I got goose-bumps all over my body when I got the call from the PGA of America," he said.

However, he knows he has a hard act to follow in Paul Azinger but, despite being his own man, Pavin is a good listener too. He has already revealed he plans to use all the positives he can from previous US Captains.

Ryder Cup experience and know-how is something that Pavin has in abundance. On the up side, he helped the United States triumph in 1991 and again at The Belfry in 1993, where he had the dubious honour of nervously hitting the first ball on the Friday morning. "Lanny Wadkins and I were paired together and I remember I had a difficult time just getting my ball onto the tee my hand was shaking so much," he said. "I was able to kind of drop it and

thank goodness it managed to stay on the tee somehow. If it hadn't, I think I would have just hit if off the ground!" On the down side, he was on the losing team at Oak Hill in 1995. He was also assistant to Tom Lehman in 2006, when the visitors were overwhelmed at The K Club in Ireland.

Whether in victory or defeat, though, Pavin is a man who always takes the positives out of everything he does. Take his first experience of Wales in 2009, for example, when he contested The Celtic Manor Wales Open on The Twenty Ten Course that will be the scene of what promises to be an epic clash.

Taking time to adapt to the conditions, he battled to make the cut right on the line but then produced a third round 71, in some of the worst of the weather, a score which was bettered by only seven of the 75 competitors who contested the weekend action.

"It was good I got to play in these conditions because you want to know how the course plays in all kinds of weather," he said. "I'll be able to tell the Team. Only trouble is, I'm not sure they'll want to hear how tough it can be!"

How tough is Pavin himself? Well, his slight physique belies a dogged disposition that is aptly shown in his nickname. You do not become the US PGA Tour Player of the Year, as he did in 1991, as a shrinking violet. You also do not win a Major Championship without

having an enduring will to beat the best, as he did in 1995, when he produced one of the most famous strokes in golf to claim the US Open Championship title. The vision of his magical four wood shot soaring nearly 230 yards to land just five feet from the pin will forever frequent the 18th hole at Shinnecock Hills alongside the spirits of the Indian Braves who once lived there.

That single shot highlights the determination and never-say-die spirit of the man. There will be no pussy-footing around by 'The Bulldog' in Wales.

Norman Dabell
Reuters

Wins Around the World

The 2009 season saw European Tour Members continue to excel not only at home, but in all four corners of the globe. In total 33 members claimed 39 titles worldwide with pride of place going to Sweden's Henrik Stenson who won The Players Championship, the flagship event on the US PGA Tour, and Germany's Bernhard Langer who captured four titles on the US Champions Tour. On these two pages are a selection of our global champions – we salute you gentlemen, one and all.

Henrik Stenson - The Players Championship

Paul Casey - Shell Houston Open

Lin Wen-tang - Mercuries Taiwan Masters

Edoardo Molinari - Dunlop Phoenix

Stephen Ames - Children's Miracle Network Classic

Peter Gustafsson - XXVI Abierto Internacional de Golf Copa Antioquia

Darren Fichardt – Nashua Masters. Darren also won the Vodacom Business Origins of Golf Tour and the Platinum Classic

Mike Harwood - Handa Australian Seniors Open

Retief Goosen - Africa Open. Retief also won the Transitions Championship

Adilson Da Silva - SAA Pro-Am Invitational

Geoff Ogilvy - Mercedes-Benz Championship

Jyoti Randhawa - Singh Thailand Open

Eduardo Romero - Toshiba Classic

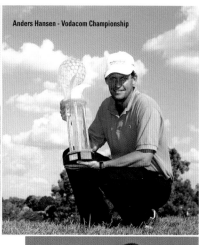
Anders Hansen - Vodacom Championship

Thaworn Wiratchant - Macau Open

Mark McNulty - Principal Charity Classic

James Kamte - Asian Tour International

Padraig Harrington -
Ladbrokes.com
Irish PGA Championship

Johan Edfors - Black Mountain Masters

Steve Alker - HSBC New Zealand PGA Championship

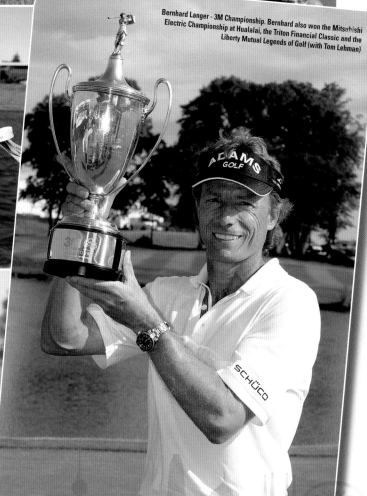
Bernhard Langer - 3M Championship. Bernhard also won the Mitsubishi Electric Championship at Hualalai, the Triton Financial Classic and the Liberty Mutual Legends of Golf (with Tom Lehman)

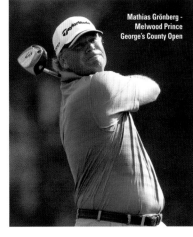
Mathias Grönberg -
Melwood Prince
George's County Open

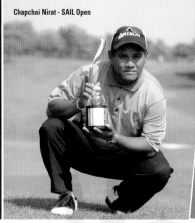
Chapchai Nirat - SAIL Open

Mission Statement

"It means the world to me. Winning the Order of Merit means I am the best Senior player in Europe this year. That feels fantastic and is right up there with the rest of the achievements in my career"

— Sam Torrance

Andy Stubbs, Managing Director of the European Senior Tour, presents the 2009 John Jacobs Trophy to Sam Torrance

When Sam Torrance won the final event of the 2008 European Senior Tour season to finish eighth on the Order of Merit, he immediately declared his intention for the new campaign – to reclaim the John Jacobs Trophy from his old friend and rival Ian Woosnam who had won it after a glorious rookie year.

Such a mission statement, from a man who had enjoyed Ryder Cup glory both as a Captain and player, was not to be taken lightly. True to his word, the Scot returned to the OKI Castellón Senior Tour Championship in 2009 and finished off the job, exactly as he had promised.

That a mere €3,380 separated Torrance and Woosnam in the closest Senior Tour Order of Merit race since 2000 was irrelevant. Torrance simply wanted to be the European Senior Tour's Number One again, three years after he last sat atop the pile.

"It means the world to me," said the 56 year old. "Winning the Order of Merit means I am the best Senior player in Europe this year. That feels fantastic and is right up there with the rest of the achievements in my career."

Ian Woosnam

Torrance's triumph is perhaps all the more satisfying given the fact that, after winning the John Jacobs Trophy for a second time in 2006, he struggled for two seasons with a hand injury. Playing through the pain, he nevertheless managed to preserve his record of winning a title in each of his full seasons on the Senior Tour since 2004 – displaying the same never say die attitude that has permeated his entire career.

"I've never been a quitter," he said. "In golf you can't be. You never know, five birdies might be just around the corner. I've always had the attitude that I'd rather finish fourth than fifth, or 41st rather than 51st."

It is that steely drive and determination to succeed that has served Torrance so well over the years since he turned professional in 1970, producing 21 European Tour titles and 11 victories on the Senior Tour. They are traits inherited from his parents June and Bob, who remain a major presence and influence in his life, and who are still regularly seen walking the fairways at tournaments the world over.

It was Bob, renowned as one of golf's great swing coaches, who nurtured Sam's game at their home in Largs, impressing on his son the same work ethic he would later hone in three-time Major Champion Padraig Harrington.

In the midst of his celebrations after winning the John Jacobs Trophy, an emotional Torrance took a moment to phone his mum and dad from the locker room at Club de Campo del Mediterráneo, acknowledging the crucial role they have played in his career.

"They were both obviously delighted and ecstatic to know that their son was the leading Senior player in Europe," he said. "My parents have given me everything. They gave me my start in golf and I wouldn't be where I am without them. My mother has been a great supporter and having my father as my coach has been fantastic. They are both my best assets."

Another major influence is his wife Suzanne, the former actress who is now the mother of his three children, and whom he memorably proposed to on board Concorde returning from Europe's victory in The 1987 Ryder Cup at Muirfield Village in Ohio.

"I'm not sure whether it was the altitude or the champagne but it was the best decision I ever made," he joked. "Suzanne has been a great supporter of mine and has helped me so much over the years."

Such displays of passion off the course have been replicated, and perhaps surpassed, on it, none more so than in The Ryder Cup arena where he

John B

Peter Mitchell

Peter Senior

Travis Perkins plc
Senior Masters

444 yds - 406 mtrs

Glenn Ralph

Delroy Cambridge

Mike Cunning

Des Smyth

Carl Mason

Roger Chapman

Mark James

Turf Equipment & Irrigation Solutions

One great result.

visit www.toro.com

 Count on it.

represented Europe eight times, holing the winning putt at The Belfry in 1985 before returning to captain the Team to victory at the same venue in 2002.

That latter achievement earned him an OBE for services to golf, a fitting tribute to a man whose appearance in the 2009 Estoril Open De Portugal on The European Tour was his 705th on the main circuit – the most of any player in history.

"That is an achievement I am very proud of," he said. "To have played more events than anyone else shows longevity and it also shows that, over the years, I must have been pretty good. I had a great career on The European Tour and my two Irish Open victories in 1981 and 1995 were probably the highlights. All your victories are special but they were particularly so, as I played so well and the crowds were magnificent – they were like Open crowds."

He twice finished second on The European Tour Order of Merit – in 1984 to Bernhard Langer and in 1995, when Colin Montgomerie prevented him from winning The Harry Vardon Trophy by making par on the last hole in the season-ending Volvo Masters.

Bertus Smit

Ross Drummond

Loren Roberts

Bob Cameron

Costantino Rocca

Flying high with the birdies and eagles.
Priceless.

www.mastercard.co.uk

EUROPEAN TOUR

PREFERRED METHOD OF PAYMENT

MasterCard

The 2009 Senior Tour campaign came down to a similarly dramatic conclusion but this time Torrance was determined not to assume the role of bridesmaid, winning the battle of the Ryder Cup Captains with his old pal Woosnam.

The Welshman had travelled to the OKI Castellón Senior Tour Championship in pole position in the Order of Merit, with Torrance, alongside Glenn Ralph and Carl Mason, poised to seize on any slip up. That seemed possible when Woosnam languished in a share of 30th place going into the final round, opening the door for Torrance who needed to finish in the top three to end the season as Number One.

However, when Woosnam produced back-to-back eagles around the turn in his final round to surge up the leaderboard it seemed as though the former World Number One might retain the John Jacobs Trophy after all.

But three costly three putts on the back nine saw the 1991 Masters Tournament Champion slip back to a share of 18th place, meaning Torrance's third place finish was sufficient to reclaim the Order of Merit crown he previously won in 2005 and 2006, as he ended the season with earnings of €170,695.

"This Order of Merit is sweeter than the other two," he said. "The older you get the harder it is. It's not like The European Tour where you are 18 or 21 and gaining experience all the time. So it was a fantastic achievement."

Having targeted the John Jacobs Trophy at the end of the 2008 season, Torrance set about making an early impression in 2009 and did just that with a share of sixth place in the Aberdeen Brunei Senior Masters presented by The Stapleford Forum before winning the DGM Barbados Open, courtesy of some scintillating golf, including a second round course record 63.

Injury problems struck again as he was forced to withdraw from both the Irish Seniors Open in association with Fáilte Ireland and AIB Bank won, ironically, by Woosnam, and The De Vere Collection PGA Seniors Championship in June but it was over his home Sunningdale Golf Club in July that he put his season back on track.

He was in contention all the way in The Senior Open Championship presented by MasterCard, eventually finishing fifth, two strokes behind winner Loren Roberts, to wrest some momentum back in the Order of Merit race from Woosnam.

Buoyed by that performance, Torrance added further top five finishes in the Bad Ragaz PGA Seniors Open and the Travis Perkins plc Senior Masters. Woosnam's fourth place in the lucrative Casa Serena Open meant he would go into the final event of the season at the helm but in an enthralling finalé, it was Torrance who

Tony Johnstone

Eamonn Darcy

Mike Harwood

edged over the line to equal Carl Mason's three Order of Merit victories, both men now just two behind Tommy Horton's record of five.

Mason, himself, had a year to remember, emerging as the only multiple winner in 2009 after his successes in The De Vere Collection PGA Seniors Championship and the inaugural Benahavis Senior Masters presented by ISPS. Not only did it help the 56 year old Englishman finish third in the Order of Merit, it also moved him to within one victory of Horton's record of 23 European Senior Tour titles.

Aside from Torrance, however, perhaps the success story of 2009 was Mason's compatriot Glenn Ralph. Having missed 14 months of golf after breaking his ankle whilst on holiday, Ralph returned in style. He won his maiden title over the Torrance-designed Fairmont St Andrews course, capturing the Cleveland Golf/Srixon Scottish Senior Open, and he also finished tied second in the Casa Serena Open en route to ending the season fourth on the Order of Merit.

Other maiden winners in 2009 were Americans Mike Cunning and Michael Allen in the Aberdeen Brunei Senior Masters presented by The Stapleford Forum and the US Senior

PGA Championship respectively; South African Bertus Smit, who won the Ryder Cup Wales Seniors Open; and Australian Mike Harwood, whose successful return to the game after a ten year break was capped by his victory in the season-ending OKI Castellón Senior Tour Championship to help him claim the Rookie of the Year Award. There were also victories for Mark James (Son Gual Mallorca Senior Open) and Delroy Cambridge (Jersey Seniors Classic).

Elsewhere, Tony Johnstone produced the season's most emotional victory, capturing the Travis Perkins plc Senior Masters the day before the Multiple Sclerosis sufferer hosted a MS Society Pro-Am at Sunningdale which raised more than £100,000.

But ultimately the year belonged to Torrance, who, like Sky Sports analyst Johnstone, is also enjoying a simultaneous career in television commentary on the BBC. The self-confessed "avid golf fan" might be reaching a new generation of followers via his work on the small screen but, as his performances on the course in 2009 showed, he is still eminently watchable himself.

Steve Todd

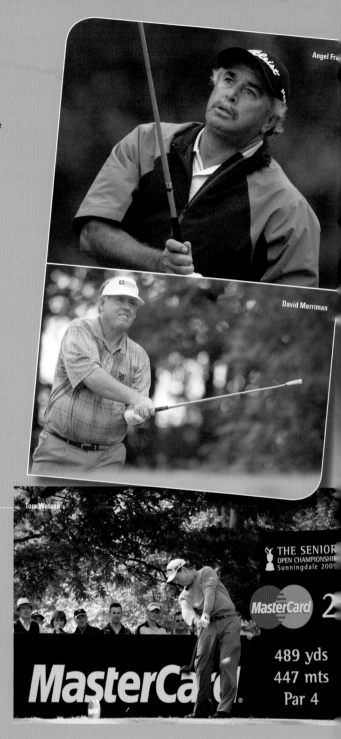

Angel Fra...

David Merriman

Tom Watson

Gordon Brand Jnr

Ian Woosnam and Sam Torrance

THE 2009 EUROPEAN SENIOR TOUR

Date		Tournament	Venue	Winner	Score	€ First Prize / Prize Fund
Feb	27-1	Aberdeen Brunei Senior Masters presented by The Stapleford Forum	The Empire Hotel & Country Club, Brunei Darussalam	**Mike Cunning, USA**	206 (-7)	€47,194 / €314,315
Mar	18-20	DGM Barbados Open	Royal Westmoreland, Barbados	**Sam Torrance, SCO**	202 (-14)	€25,234 / €160,105
May	8-10	Son Gual Mallorca Senior Open	Son Gual Golf, Palma, Mallorca, Spain	**Mark James, ENG****	206 (-10)	€45,000 / €299,700
	21-24	US Senior PGA Championship	Canterbury GC, Beachwood, Ohio, USA	**Michael Allen, USA**	274 (-6)	€266,528 / €1,516,949
Jun	5-7	Irish Seniors Open in association with Fáilte Ireland and AIB Bank	Ballybunion Golf Club, Co. Kerry, Ireland	**Ian Woosnam, WAL**,**	211 (-2)	€52,500 / €349,284
	12-14	Jersey Seniors Classic	La Moye GC, Jersey, Channel Islands	**Delroy Cambridge, JAM****	207 (-9)	€24,394 / €160,091
	19-21	Ryder Cup Wales Seniors Open	Royal Porthcawl GC, Mid Glamorgan, Wales	**Bertus Smit, RSA**	211 (-5)	€88,234 / €588,230
	25-28	The De Vere Collection PGA Seniors Championship	Hunting Course, De Vere Slaley Hall, Northumberland, England	**Carl Mason, ENG**	279 (-9)	€47,115 / €294,470
Jul	23-26	The Senior Open Championship presented by MasterCard	Sunningdale GC (Old Course), Berkshire, England	**Loren Roberts, USA****	268 (-12)	€222,777/€1,414,914
	30-2	US Senior Open*	Crooked Stick GC, Carmel, Indiana, USA	**Fred Funk, USA**	268 (-20)	$470,000 / $2,600,000
Aug	7-9	Bad Ragaz PGA Seniors Open	Golf Club Bad Ragaz, Switzerland	**John Bland, RSA****	199 (-11)	€33,000 / €220,407
	21-23	Cleveland Golf / Srixon Scottish Senior Open	Fairmont St. Andrews, Fife, Scotland	**Glenn Ralph, ENG**	208 (-8)	€39,353 / €262,094
Sept	4-6	Travis Perkins plc Senior Masters	Duke's Course, Woburn GC, England	**Tony Johnstone, ZIM**	206 (-10)	€42,781 / €285,210
	18-20	Casa Serena Open	Casa Serena Golf, Kutna Hora, Czech Republic	**Peter Mitchell, ENG**	200 (-13)	€90,000 / €600,000
Oct	16-18	Benahavis Senior Masters presented by ISPS	La Quinta G&CC, Marbella, Spain	**Carl Mason, ENG**	206 (-7)	€27,000 / €180,000
Nov	6-8	OKI Castellón Senior Tour Championship	Club de Campo del Mediterráneo, Castellón, Spain	**Mike Harwood, AUS**	203 (-13)	€64,433 / €400,000
	12-13	EST Qualifying School Stage One	Silves Golf and Gramacho, Pestana Golf Resort, Algarve, Portugal	**65 Qualifiers for the Final Stage**		
	16-19	Senior Tour Qualifying School Final	Vale de Pinta, Pestana Golf Resort, Portugal	**John Harrison, ENG**	270 (-14)	€3,927 / €23,002

* Money won does not count towards the European Senior Tour Order of Merit

** Denotes play-off

THE 2009 EUROPEAN SENIOR TOUR ORDER OF MERIT

Pos	Name	Country	Played	€	Pos	Name	Country	Played	€
1	Sam TORRANCE	(SCO)	(14)	170695.55	57	Guillermo ENCINA	(CHI)	(11)	17527.49
2	Ian WOOSNAM	(WAL)	(13)	167315.64	58	Jeff HALL	(ENG)	(12)	15899.25
3	Carl MASON	(ENG)	(12)	157917.95	59	Denis DURNIAN	(ENG)	(12)	14378.04
4	Glenn RALPH	(ENG)	(14)	150723.46	+60	Marc FARRY	(FRA)	(5)	14077.79
5	Angel FRANCO	(PAR)	(14)	136466.88	61	Alan TAPIE	(USA)	(5)	13954.05
6	Peter MITCHELL	(ENG)	(13)	128044.82	+62	Greg TOWNE	(USA)	(9)	12743.63
7	Tony JOHNSTONE	(ZIM)	(13)	124990.80	+63	George RYALL	(ENG)	(6)	12537.75
8	Bob CAMERON	(ENG)	(15)	124686.30	64	Terry GALE	(AUS)	(10)	10439.04
+9	Mike HARWOOD	(AUS)	(14)	120231.75	65	Jeff HAWKES	(RSA)	(8)	10357.34
10	Bertus SMIT	(RSA)	(14)	116656.02	66	Ian MOSEY	(ENG)	(12)	10172.75
11	Ross DRUMMOND	(SCO)	(14)	97920.26	67	Martin POXON	(ENG)	(9)	9458.94
+12	Roger CHAPMAN	(ENG)	(13)	97663.36	68	Tony ALLEN	(ENG)	(7)	9292.75
13	David MERRIMAN	(AUS)	(13)	97506.08	69	Mike MILLER	(SCO)	(12)	9072.63
+14	Peter SENIOR	(AUS)	(3)	93950.62	70	Bob CHARLES	(NZL)	(6)	8352.58
15	Des SMYTH	(IRL)	(12)	93452.60	71	Maurice BEMBRIDGE	(ENG)	(11)	8198.71
+16	Gordon BRAND JNR	(SCO)	(12)	92002.13	72	Alfonso BARRERA	(ARG)	(10)	7949.01
17	Nick JOB	(ENG)	(15)	91985.59	73	Gery WATINE	(FRA)	(10)	7833.04
18	Bob BOYD	(USA)	(13)	88321.50	74	José Maria CAÑIZARES	(ESP)	(5)	7591.32
+19	Chris WILLIAMS	(RSA)	(8)	82499.60	75	Antonio GARRIDO	(ESP)	(12)	7574.76
20	Jerry BRUNER	(USA)	(16)	82071.74	+76	Peter FOWLER	(AUS)	(4)	7470.55
21	Gordon J BRAND	(ENG)	(16)	73042.79	+77	Peter ALLAN	(ENG)	(5)	6955.40
22	José RIVERO	(ESP)	(11)	72701.99	+78	Per-Arne BROSTEDT	(SWE)	(9)	6609.44
23	Eamonn DARCY	(IRL)	(11)	71111.95	79	John HOSKISON	(ENG)	(7)	6391.13
24	Bobby LINCOLN	(RSA)	(14)	69859.94	80	Tony CHARNLEY	(ENG)	(8)	5934.91
25	Domingo HOSPITAL	(ESP)	(13)	66743.33	81	Victor GARCIA	(ESP)	(8)	5469.74
26	John BLAND	(RSA)	(8)	65742.85	82	Graham BANISTER	(AUS)	(4)	4886.64
27	Jimmy HEGGARTY	(NIR)	(15)	63476.46	83	Eddie POLLAND	(NIR)	(10)	4853.56
28	Katsuyoshi TOMORI	(JPN)	(9)	60318.21	84	Philippe DUGENY	(FRA)	(4)	4413.10
29	John CHILLAS	(SCO)	(14)	59067.74	85	Philip HARRISON	(ENG)	(2)	4016.16
30	Bill LONGMUIR	(SCO)	(15)	58584.15	86	Jean Pierre SALLAT	(FRA)	(2)	3522.00
31	Kevin SPURGEON	(ENG)	(14)	58423.40	87	Peter TERAVAINEN	(USA)	(4)	3459.18
32	Giuseppe CALI	(ITA)	(13)	58279.85	88	Greg HOPKINS	(USA)	(5)	3293.39
33	Delroy CAMBRIDGE	(JAM)	(14)	57510.53	89	Matt BRIGGS	(ENG)	(4)	2964.72
34	Denis O'SULLIVAN	(IRL)	(14)	53913.26	90	Bill MCCOLL	(SCO)	(2)	2708.81
35	Juan QUIROS	(ESP)	(13)	51826.79	91	John BENDA	(USA)	(2)	2225.02
+36	Mike CUNNING	(USA)	(14)	50891.36	92	Jim LAPSLEY	(NZL)	(4)	2093.26
37	Luis CARBONETTI	(ARG)	(15)	50684.97	93	Ian PALMER	(RSA)	(1)	1877.93
38	Mike CLAYTON	(AUS)	(10)	47319.43	94	Steve STULL	(USA)	(3)	1807.89
39	Emilio RODRIGUEZ	(ESP)	(11)	44861.26	95	Peter O'HAGAN	(IRL)	(3)	1743.06
40	Andrew MURRAY	(ENG)	(13)	44345.44	96	Bob LARRATT	(ENG)	(3)	1634.60
41	Costantino ROCCA	(ITA)	(12)	44110.18	97	Ray CARRASCO	(USA)	(2)	1483.55
42	Noel RATCLIFFE	(AUS)	(9)	38967.63	98	Steve MARTIN	(SCO)	(1)	1348.67
43	David J RUSSELL	(ENG)	(13)	38227.79	99	Peter DAHLBERG	(SWE)	(2)	1129.42
44	Horacio CARBONETTI	(ARG)	(11)	37877.77	100	Tim RASTALL	(ENG)	(2)	995.31
45	Doug JOHNSON	(USA)	(13)	37360.15	101	Juan ANGLADA	(ESP)	(1)	864.00
46	Torsten GIEDEON	(GER)	(11)	33912.95	102	Bill HARDWICK	(CAN)	(3)	802.75
47	Seiji EBIHARA	(JPN)	(5)	33583.86	103	Dewey ARNETTE	(USA)	(1)	790.69
48	Manuel PIÑERO	(ESP)	(11)	26617.08	104	Richard MASTERS	(ENG)	(2)	705.89
49	Stewart GINN	(AUS)	(8)	23604.72	105	Glyn DAVIES	(WAL)	(2)	676.46
50	Angel FERNANDEZ	(CHI)	(12)	21949.97	106	Carlsen LEACOCK	(BAR)	(1)	622.46
51	Pete OAKLEY	(USA)	(14)	21451.15	107	Adan SOWA	(ARG)	(1)	503.41
52	David GOOD	(AUS)	(11)	20565.45	108	Bruce HEUCHAN	(CAN)	(1)	378.00
53	Simon OWEN	(NZL)	(10)	20416.87	109	Brian JONES	(AUS)	(1)	361.82
54	Jim RHODES	(ENG)	(11)	19906.83	110	Barrie STEVENS	(ENG)	(2)	315.00
55	Mike WILLIAMS	(ZIM)	(12)	19819.04	111	Tony PRICE	(WAL)	(2)	264.00
+56	Stephen BENNETT	(ENG)	(11)	18666.46	+ Denotes Rookie				

203

Italian Flair

Back row L-R: Carlos Rodiles, Chris Gane, Andrew Tampion, John Parry, Julien Guerrier, Andrew McArthur, James Morrison, Sion Bebb, François Calmels
Front row L-R: Peter Baker, Robert Coles, José-Filipe Lima, Nicolas Colsaerts, Rhys Davies, Peter Whiteford, Edoardo Molinari, Andrew Butterfield, Gary Boyd, Julien Quesne, Richard McEvoy

The 2009 Challenge Tour season will be remembered chiefly for the sheer dominance of one man: Edoardo Molinari. From the very first event of the season, the Club Colombia Masters presentado por Samsung where he finished second behind winner Alan Wagner of Argentina, the Italian never once slipped out of the top five of the Challenge Tour Rankings.

José-Filipe Lima

Having ascended to the Number One position at the beginning of August on the back of another runner-up finish in the Scottish Hydro Challenge, this time behind home favourite Jamie McLeary, he never looked like loosening his grip on the top spot. Everyone else was merely playing for a place in the top 20 to guarantee a card for The 2010 European Tour International Schedule.

In between those two second places was his first Challenge Tour title of the season and first on home soil, in the Piemonte Open at Golf Club La Mandria in Turin, which he led from start to finish.

He would later add the Kazakhstan Open at the Zhailjau Golf Resort in Almaty and the Italian Federation Cup at Olgiata Golf Club in Rome to smash the Challenge Tour record for earnings in a sensational season which also saw him climb an incredible 569 places to 84th on the Official World Golf Ranking. Furthermore, three weeks after he secured the Number One spot, Molinari overcame Robert Karlsson in a play-off for the Dunlop Phoenix in Japan with which he climbed to 63rd on the Official World Golf Ranking.

Thus, the man friends call 'Dodo', has shown he is very much alive and kicking after a brief lull in a career which seemed destined for greatness when he burst onto the amateur scene as a fresh-faced youngster.

After winning the US Amateur Championship in 2005, most golf sages predicted the young Italian would go on to take the professional game by storm. Then, when he won in Colombia on his first appearance on the Challenge Tour as a professional in 2007, that view merely hardened.

Another victory in the Tusker Kenya Open just three events later confirmed his latent promise and helped propel

him towards The European Tour, from whence few judges expected him to return. But those judges were wrong. Perhaps everything in his fledgling career had come a little too easily?

Whatever the reasons, 2008 proved to be something of a struggle for Molinari and he lost his card after a season in which his highest finish was 15th in the South African Airways Open. It had been a chastening experience for a player whose career, until then, had only been on an upward trajectory.

The setback might have caused irreparable damage to the confidence of lesser players but over the winter months he ripped up the script, started again with a new swing under the watchful eye of his coach and Sky Sports Golf Night analyst Denis Pugh, and worked harder than ever to iron out the flaws in his game.

The results, as everyone has seen, have been spectacular. If how you react to

Nicolas Colsaerts

Rhys Davies

Peter Whiteford
Rhys Davies

Peter Baker

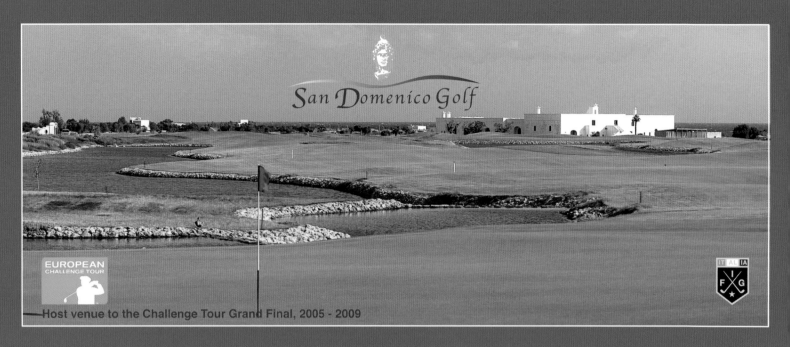

San Domenico Golf

Host venue to the Challenge Tour Grand Final, 2005 - 2009

72010 Savelletri di Fasano (BR) - Puglia - ITALY   Tel. +39 (0)80 4829200 - Fax +39 (0)80 4827944
e-mail: info@sandomenicogolf.com   www.sandomenicogolf.com

Borgo Egnazia
HOTEL VILLAS GOLF SPA

www.borgoegnazia.com.

72010 Savelletri di Fasano (BR) - Puglia - ITALY   Tel. +39 (0)80 4827886 - Fax +39 (0)80 4827950
e-mail: info@masseriacimino.com   www.masseriacimino.com

adversity is a true test of a man's mettle, then Molinari has passed with flying colours. During a season in which he missed just one cut, Molinari finished in the top ten on no fewer than 12 occasions to end the year as the undisputed Number One with record earnings of €242,979, some €98,861 more than the previous record holder, the 2008 Challenge Tour winner David Horsey.

Indeed, the figure was just short of the one needed to keep your card in The 2009 Race to Dubai on The European Tour International Schedule which, given the difference between the prize funds available on the two Tours, further illustrates his exceptional achievement.

Now, confidence fully restored, and with a brand new sports car in the garage as a reward for his exploits, Molinari can plan a second assault on The European Tour next season alongside younger brother Francesco, completing a golfing journey which began at their local golf club in Turin.

From an early age, the two brothers would compete with one another and Edoardo, being the elder by two years, would invariably claim the bragging rights.

"We are competitive, as all brothers naturally are," he said. "But we're also very happy when the other brother plays well. In the main we have a very good relationship, because we were very close when we were growing up. I was probably five or six years old when I first picked up a golf club. My father played and he used to take me and Francesco with him sometimes.

"Then when I was about 12 or 13 we started taking golf a little more seriously, and entered some junior competitions. I got into the National Team when I was 15, and I won the Italian Amateur Championship in 2001. Francesco won the Italian Amateur Stroke Play Championship the next year, and we won the Italian Amateur Foursomes Championship together, so we

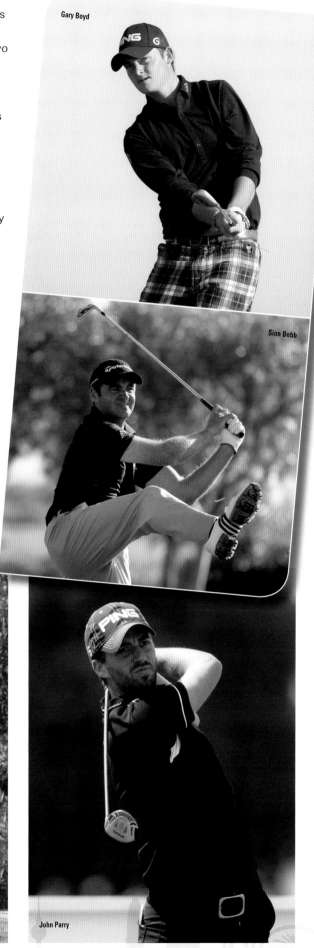
Gary Boyd

Sion Bebb

John Parry

Julien Quesne

Andrew Tampion

François Calmels

Chris Gane

were both playing at a high level. Because I was older I was probably hitting the ball a bit further and playing a bit better, so he was always trying to catch me up. But now it's the other way round!

"He's had a fantastic season, and he's moved into the top 50 in the world for the first time in his career which, if he stays there, would get him into the Majors next season. I think his game is perfectly suited to Major Championships because from tee to green he's probably as good as anyone out there. I think he's definitely ready to win again soon."

Indeed, Francesco's form is such that he is a contender to make The Ryder Cup Team at The Celtic Manor Resort next

year, and alongside Edoardo will be seeking to follow in the footsteps of Costantino Rocca who became, to date, the only Italian to play in the biennial contest at The Belfry in 1993, at Oak Hill Country Club in 1995 and Club de Golf Valderrama in 1997.

Both brothers idolised Rocca as youngsters and Edoardo, having previously played alongside his hero at the 2006 Italian Open, recently chewed the fat with the veteran. "I was lucky enough to play with Costantino a few times before he moved onto the Senior Tour and it was a real privilege to meet one of my heroes," he said.

"He's such a great guy, both on and off the course – a true gentleman. The day after my win in Rome, I had breakfast with him because he was doing a coaching clinic for children at the same course. It was great to catch up with him – he's always great company. He was on Tour for more than 20 years and played in The Ryder Cup, so he's always got some great stories to tell. What he did for golf in Italy was huge, and hopefully I too can inspire some more young Italians to play the game."

Joining the Italian duo on The European Tour will be Portugal's José-Filipe Lima, who finished some €108,358 behind Molinari in second place on the Rankings, but who owed his high finish largely to his first Challenge Tour victory in five years in the ECCO Tour Championship in October and a runner-up finish behind Sweden's Christian Nilsson in the dual ranking SAINT-OMER OPEN presented by Neuflize OBC in June.

Directly behind Lima in the Rankings came Belgium's Nicolas Colsaerts and Welshman Rhys Davies who, along with England's Robert Coles, claimed two titles apiece.

A rejuvenated Colsaerts, who began the season without a Challenge Tour category, finally began to fulfil some of his undoubted promise with victories in the SK Golf Challenge in August and in The Dutch Futures a month later.

At the other end of the experience spectrum, Davies continued the form which had seen him claim ten titles on the American collegiate circuit with victories on home soil in the SWALEC Wales Challenge in July and in foreign climes in September in the Fred Olsen Challenge de España.

Meanwhile Coles, a winner of the Moroccan Classic by BANQUE POPULAIRE in April and the Challenge of Ireland presented by Moyvalley in June, had looked on course to capture a third Challenge Tour title of the season – and therefore claim automatic promotion to The European Tour – when he raced into a three stroke lead at the halfway stage of the Trophée du Golf de Genève in mid August.

Richard McEvoy

Carlos Rodiles

Andrew Butterfield

But in running to the aid of Lima, who had lost his ball on an adjacent fairway, the unfortunate Englishman injured his calf muscle and had to withdraw from the event, which was instead won on his 29th birthday by Frenchman Julien Quesne.

Quesne eventually graduated to The European Tour in eighth place in the Rankings, along with his fellow 2009 Challenge Tour champions: Englishmen Peter Baker (Credit Suisse Challenge), Gary Boyd (Tusker Kenya Open 2009), Andrew Butterfield (The Princess) and John Parry (ALLIANZ Golf Open Grand Toulouse), Frenchman François Calmels (Telenet Trophy) and Peter Whiteford of Scotland who moved up from 15th to finish fifth following his victory in the season-ending Apulia San Domenico Grand Final in Puglia, Italy.

They will be joined on The 2010 Race to Dubai by their fellow graduates Sion Bebb of Wales (19th), the English trio of Chris Gane (13th), Richard McEvoy (ninth) and James Morrison (18th), Frenchman Julien Guerrier (16th), Scotland's Andrew McArthur (17th), Spain's Carlos Rodiles (12th) and Andrew Tampion of Australia

(15th), all of whom were rewarded for their steadiness throughout the season.

Finally, evidence of the growing strength in depth of the European Challenge Tour was provided by the fact that five players – Christoph Günther of Germany (Kärnten Golf Open presented by Markus Brier Foundation), Lee James of England (ALLIANZ Open Côtes d'Armor Bretagne), Alexandre Kaleka of France (ALLIANZ EurOpen de Lyon), Scotland's Eric Ramsay (DHL Wroclaw Open) and Alan Wagner (Club Colombia Masters presentado por Samsung) – all won during 2009 but did not produce consistency enough elsewhere to finish in the top 20 of the Rankings. But with both time and talent on their side, another chance to take the step up to The European Tour will surely not be long in coming.

Paul Symes

Below Challenge Tour Director, Alain de Soultrait, congratulates Rankings winner Edoardo Molinari

Julien Guerrier

Andrew McArthur

Robert Coles

James Morrison

THE 2009 EUROPEAN CHALLENGE TOUR

Date		Tournament	Venue	Winner	Score	€ First Prize/Prize Fund
Mar	19 - 22	Club Colombia Masters presentado por Samsung	Country Club de Bogotá, Bogotá, Colombia	**Alan Wagner ARG**	275 (-13)	€24,802 / €155,014
Apr	16 - 19	Tusker Kenya Open 2009	Muthaiga GC, Nairobi, Kenya	**Gary Boyd ENG**	271 (-13)	€28,800 / €184,662
	30 - 03	Moroccan Classic by BANQUE POPULAIRE	Pullman El Jadida Royal Golf and Spa, El Jadida, Morocco	**Robert Coles, ENG**	275 (-13)	€22,400 / €144,396
May	14 - 17	ALLIANZ Open Côtes d'Armor Bretagne	Golf Blue Green de Pléneuf Val André, France	**Lee James, ENG****	274 (-6)	€24,000 / €154,410
	20 - 23	Piemonte Open	GC La Mandria, Torino, Italy	**Edoardo Molinari ITA**	270 (-18)	€24,000 / €150,885
	28 - 31	Telenet Trophy	Royal Waterloo, La Marache Course, Lasne, Belgium	**François Calmels FRA**	276 (-12)	€24,000 / €154,410
June	04 - 07	Kärnten Golf Open presented by Markus Brier Foundation	Golf Club Klagenfurt-Seltenheim, Carinthia, Austria	**Christoph Günther GER**	268 (-20)	€22,400 / €142,646
	11 - 14	Challenge of Ireland presented by Moyvalley	The Champions Club, Moyvalley Hotel & Country Club, Co. Kildare, Ireland	**Robert Coles ENG****	278 (-10)	€24,000 / €156,100
	18 - 21	SAINT-OMER OPEN presented by Neuflize OBC	Aa St Omer GC, Lumbres, France	**Christian Nilsson, SWE**	271 (-13)	€83,333 / €606,240*
	25 - 28	The Princess	Båstad GK, Båstal, Sweden	**Andrew Butterfield, ENG**	271 (-13)	€48,000 / €305,760
July	02 - 05	Credit Suisse Challenge	Wylihof GC, Luterbach, Switzerland	**Peter Baker, ENG**	274 (-18)	€22,400 / €142,310
	09 - 12	ALLIANZ EurOpen de Lyon	Golf du Gouverneur, Monthieux, France	**Alexandre Kaleka, FRA**	268 (-16)	€24,000 / €155,460
	23 - 26	SWALEC Wales Challenge	Vale Hotel Golf & Spa Resort, Cardiff, Wales	**Rhys Davies, WAL****	286 (-2)	€24,000 / €152,475
	30 - 02	Scottish Hydro Challenge	Macdonald Spey Valley GC, Aviemore, Scotland	**Jamie McLeary, SCO**	276 (-8)	€32,000 / €203,300
Aug	06 - 09	SK Golf Challenge	Linna GC, Vanajanlinna, Finland	**Nicolas Colsaerts****, BEL	277 (-11)	€28,000 / €179,095
	13 - 16	Trophée du Golf de Genève	Golf de Genève, Genève, Switzerland	**Julien Quesne, FRA**	269 (-19)	€24,400 / €210,000
	27 - 30	DHL Wroclaw Open	Toya G&CC, Wroclaw, Poland	**Eric Ramsay, SCO**	263 (-17)	€22,400 / €143,276
Sept	03 - 06	Fred Olsen Challenge de España	Tecina Golf, La Gomera, Canary Islands, Spain	**Rhys Davies, WAL**	267 (-17)	€24,000 / €153,825
	10 - 13	The Dutch Futures	GC Houtrak, Halfweg, The Netherlands	**Nicolas Colsaerts, BEL**	271 (-17)	€24,000 / €150,885
	17 - 20	Kazakhstan Open	Zhailjau Golf Resort, Almaty, Kazakhstan	**Edoardo Molinari, ITA**	268 (-20)	€64,000 / €405,600
	24 - 27	Omega Mission Hills World Cup Qualifier	Estonian Golf & Country Club, Jõelähtme Parish, Estonia	**Canada**	269 (-19)	
Oct	01 - 04	ECCO Tour Championship	Holstebro GK, Jutland, Denmark	**José-Filipe Lima, POR**	211 (-5) (54holes)	€28,800 / €182,052
	08 - 11	ALLIANZ Golf Open Grand Toulouse	Golf de Toulouse Seilh, Seilh, France	**John Parry, ENG**	267 (-21)	€24,000 / €152,100
	21 - 24	Italian Federation Cup	Olgiata GC, Rome, Italy	**Edoardo Molinari, ITA**	267 (-21)	€24,000 / €150,450
	28 - 31	Apulia San Domenico Grand Final	San Domenico Golf, Puglia, Italy	**Peter Whiteford, SCO****	279 (-5)	€51,500 / €300,000

* Dual ranking event, for Ranking point purposes the prize fund will be capped at €500,000
** Denotes play-off

THE 2009 EUROPEAN CHALLENGE TOUR RANKINGS

Pos	Name	Country	Played	€	Pos	Name	Country	Played	€
1	**Edoardo MOLINARI**	(ITA)	(19)	**242979.53**	51	Simon THORNTON	(IRL)	(12)	24737.50
2	**José-Filipe LIMA**	(POR)	(15)	**134622.50**	52	Colm MORIARTY	(IRL)	(18)	24155.38
3	**Nicolas COLSAERTS**	(BEL)	(20)	**128590.00**	53	Julien CLÉMENT	(SUI)	(14)	24089.96
4	**Rhys DAVIES**	(WAL)	(12)	**113187.38**	54	Ben EVANS	(ENG)	(21)	24050.00
5	**Peter WHITEFORD**	(SCO)	(20)	**110592.82**	55	George MURRAY	(SCO)	(18)	24030.67
6	**Andrew BUTTERFIELD**	(ENG)	(21)	**110487.67**	56	Julien GRILLON	(FRA)	(22)	23762.97
7	**Gary BOYD**	(ENG)	(18)	**104952.33**	57	Philip GOLDING	(ENG)	(12)	23185.00
8	**Julien QUESNE**	(FRA)	(23)	**94635.52**	58	Garry HOUSTON	(WAL)	(19)	22437.08
9	**Richard MCEVOY**	(ENG)	(21)	**92919.02**	59	Steve SURRY	(ENG)	(9)	22363.33
10	**Robert COLES**	(ENG)	(19)	**89304.45**	60	Antti AHOKAS	(FIN)	(13)	22088.04
11	**Peter BAKER**	(ENG)	(16)	**74243.42**	61	Mark F HAASTRUP	(DEN)	(19)	21795.51
12	**Carlos RODILES**	(ESP)	(13)	**73898.19**	62	Thorbjorn OLESEN	(DEN)	(9)	21646.67
13	**Chris GANE**	(ENG)	(19)	**73230.38**	63	Andreas HÖGBERG	(SWE)	(18)	21099.93
14	**John PARRY**	(ENG)	(19)	**71318.33**	64	Benjamin HEBERT	(FRA)	(14)	20571.43
15	**Andrew TAMPION**	(AUS)	(17)	**65415.50**	65	Ben MASON	(ENG)	(17)	20399.73
16	**Julien GUERRIER**	(FRA)	(22)	**64740.68**	66	Christophe BRAZILLIER	(FRA)	(21)	19961.17
17	**Andrew MCARTHUR**	(SCO)	(22)	**62855.76**	67	Federico COLOMBO	(ITA)	(16)	18568.00
18	**James MORRISON**	(ENG)	(21)	**61370.29**	68	Roope KAKKO	(FIN)	(9)	18552.50
19	**Sion BEBB**	(WAL)	(16)	**61231.33**	69	Clodomiro CARRANZA	(ARG)	(17)	18544.17
20	**François CALMELS**	(FRA)	(23)	**58919.83**	70	Nicolas MEITINGER	(GER)	(20)	18323.50
21	Peter GUSTAFSSON	(SWE)	(20)	55370.23	71	Scott JAMIESON	(SCO)	(10)	18298.33
22	Christoph GÜNTHER	(GER)	(21)	54722.36	72	Thomas FEYRSINGER	(AUT)	(14)	18176.50
23	Alan WAGNER	(ARG)	(20)	50312.39	73	Andrew WILLEY	(ENG)	(18)	17971.88
24	Jamie MCLEARY	(SCO)	(19)	50287.00	74	Steven TILEY	(ENG)	(6)	17970.00
25	Fredrik ANDERSSON HED	(SWE)	(10)	48464.38	75	Nathan SMITH	(USA)	(14)	17534.00
26	Alexandre KALEKA	(FRA)	(12)	48276.00	76	Peter KAENSCHE	(NOR)	(14)	17491.22
27	Matthew ZIONS	(AUS)	(21)	48055.42	77	Tony CAROLAN	(AUS)	(7)	17288.80
28	Roland STEINER	(AUT)	(21)	47240.75	78	Stuart DAVIS	(ENG)	(8)	17183.00
29	Lee S JAMES	(ENG)	(23)	41410.67	79	Jesus Maria ARRUTI	(ESP)	(13)	16957.00
30	Oscar FLOREN	(SWE)	(19)	40433.42	80	Victor RIU	(FRA)	(20)	16619.50
31	Florian FRITSCH	(GER)	(14)	40084.19	81	Adrien BERNADET	(FRA)	(22)	16195.35
32	Sam WALKER	(ENG)	(14)	38846.48	82	Matthew CORT	(ENG)	(11)	15901.25
33	Gareth PADDISON	(NZL)	(16)	38367.21	83	Jamie MOUL	(ENG)	(16)	15854.51
34	Steven JEPPESEN	(SWE)	(21)	37914.33	84	Ricardo SANTOS	(POR)	(19)	15842.67
35	Eric RAMSAY	(SCO)	(19)	37539.50	85	Marcus HIGLEY	(ENG)	(10)	15674.50
36	Andrew MARSHALL	(ENG)	(17)	37300.83	86	Julio ZAPATA	(ARG)	(12)	15465.76
37	Anders Schmidt HANSEN	(DEN)	(22)	37252.50	87	Juan ABBATE	(ARG)	(12)	15195.56
38	Stuart MANLEY	(WAL)	(14)	36193.64	88	Soren JUUL	(DEN)	(13)	15188.76
39	Martin WIEGELE	(AUT)	(18)	35212.83	89	Liam BOND	(WAL)	(19)	15054.29
40	Lorenzo GAGLI	(ITA)	(14)	33905.83	90	David GRIFFITHS	(ENG)	(14)	14679.38
41	Åke NILSSON	(SWE)	(10)	33303.00	91	Joel SJÖHOLM	(SWE)	(17)	14371.11
42	Florian PRAEGANT	(AUT)	(20)	32737.75	92	Daniel DENISON	(ENG)	(12)	14304.50
43	Javier COLOMO	(ESP)	(18)	31732.00	93	Tom WHITEHOUSE	(ENG)	(18)	13195.75
44	Mark TULLO	(CHI)	(18)	31007.32	94	David HEWAN	(RSA)	(6)	12923.75
45	Adam GEE	(ENG)	(20)	30225.92	95	Greig HUTCHEON	(SCO)	(9)	12272.00
46	Carl SUNESON	(ESP)	(18)	26821.95	96	Lloyd SALTMAN	(SCO)	(17)	12108.75
47	Jan-Are LARSEN	(NOR)	(18)	26568.42	97	Gregory MOLTENI	(ITA)	(19)	12054.50
48	Charles-Edouard RUSSO	(FRA)	(18)	26507.00	98	Jorge CAMPILLO	(ESP)	(5)	11875.00
49	Lloyd KENNEDY	(ENG)	(18)	26030.13	99	Björn PETTERSSON	(SWE)	(15)	11571.55
50	Mikko KORHONEN	(FIN)	(14)	25508.25	100	Jean-Nicolas BILLOT	(FRA)	(17)	10931.54

Rory McIlroy - January   **Geoff Ogilvy** - February   **Søren Kjeldsen** - March   **Angel Cabrera with George O'Grady** - April

THE 2009 RACE TO DUBAI EUROPEAN TOUR GOLFER OF THE MONTH AWARDS

The Race to Dubai European Tour Golfer of the Month Awards are presented throughout the year followed by an Annual Award. The winners receive an engraved alms dish and a jeroboam of Moët & Chandon champagne

ANNUAL WINNERS

2009	Lee Westwood	1996	Colin Montgomerie
2008	Padraig Harrington	1995	Colin Montgomerie
2007	Padraig Harrington	1994	Ernie Els
2006	Paul Casey	1993	Bernhard Langer
2005	Michael Campbell	1992	Nick Faldo
2004	Vijay Singh	1991	Severiano Ballesteros
2003	Ernie Els	1990	Nick Faldo
2002	Ernie Els	1989	Nick Faldo
2001	Retief Goosen	1988	Severiano Ballesteros
2000	Lee Westwood	1987	Ian Woosnam
1999	Colin Montgomerie	1986	Severiano Ballesteros
1998	Lee Westwood	1985	Bernhard Langer
1997	Colin Montgomerie		

Lee Westwood - August, November and The 2009 Race to Dubai European Tour Golfer of the Year

Shane Lowry - May   **Nick Dougherty** - June   **Martin Kaymer** - July   **Rafael Cabrera-Bello** - September   **Ross Fisher** - October

Rory McIlroy with Keith Waters - January and March

Paul Casey - February and May

Angel Cabrera - April

THE 2009 EUROPEAN TOUR SHOT OF THE MONTH AWARDS

The European Tour Shot of the Month Awards are presented throughout the year followed by an Annual Award

ANNUAL WINNERS

2008	Padraig Harrington	
2007	Angel Cabrera	
2006	Paul Casey	
2005	Paul McGinley	
2004	David Howell	
2003	Fredrik Jacobson	

Rafa Echenique with David Williams - June

Ricardo Gonzalez - July

Alex Noren - August and September

Lee Westwood with Richard Hills - October

DIRECTORS

N C Coles, MBE, Chairman

A Gallardo, Vice Chairman

M Bembridge

P Eales

C Hanell

D Jones

R Lee

J E O'Leary

M Roe

D J Russell

O Sellberg

J Spence

Sir M F Bonallack, OBE
(Non Executive Tour Group Director)

P A T Davidson
(Non Executive Tour Group Director, Finance)

B Nordberg
(Non Executive Tour Group Director)

N Northridge
(Non Executive Tour Group Director)

K S Owen
(Non Executive Tour Group Director, Broadcasting)

CHIEF EXECUTIVE	G C O'Grady
DIRECTOR OF INTERNATIONAL POLICY	K Waters
RYDER CUP DIRECTOR	R G Hills
FINANCIAL DIRECTOR & COMPANY SECRETARY	J Orr
GROUP MARKETING DIRECTOR	S F Kelly
DIRECTOR OF CORPORATE AFFAIRS AND PUBLIC RELATIONS	M S Platts
DIRECTOR OF TOUR OPERATIONS	D W Garland
DIRECTOR OF BROADCASTING & NEW MEDIA	M Lichtenhein
DIRECTOR OF PROPERTY AND VENUE DEVELOPMENT	D MacLaren
MANAGING DIRECTOR, EUROPEAN SENIOR TOUR	K A Stubbs
DIRECTOR OF CHALLENGE TOUR	A de Soultrait
CHIEF REFEREE	J N Paramor
ASSISTANT DIRECTOR OF TOUR OPERATIONS	D A Probyn
SENIOR REFEREE	A N McFee
SENIOR TOURNAMENT DIRECTOR AND QUALIFYING SCHOOL DIRECTOR	M R Stewart
DIRECTOR OF INTERNATIONAL CHAMPIONSHIPS	P Adams
DIRECTOR OF CHAMPIONSHIP MANAGEMENT	J Birkmyre
RYDER CUP MATCH DIRECTOR	E Kitson
SALES DIRECTOR	T Shaw
DIRECTOR OF COMMUNICATIONS	G Simpson

PHOTOGRAPHERS

gettyimages®

David Cannon
Tom Dulat
Julian Finney
Stuart Franklin
Sam Greenwood
Scott Halleran
Richard Heathcote
Harry How
Phil Inglis
Ross Kinnaird
Warren Little
Andy Lyons
Ryan Pierse
Andrew Redington
Jamie Squire
Michael Steele
Ian Walton

ADDITIONAL CONTRIBUTORS

Asian Tour
Mercuries
Montana Pritchard
PGA of America
SAIL
Sunshine Tour
USGA/John Mummert
World Golf Hall of Fame
World Sport Group

TOURNAMENT COMMITTEE

T Björn (DEN)

P Casey (ENG)

D Clarke (NIR)

G Fernandez-Castaño (ESP)

R Finch (ENG)

J Haeggman (SWE)

D Howell (ENG)

R Jacquelin (FRA)

M A Jiménez (ESP)

R Karlsson (SWE)

B Lane (ENG)

Paul Lawrie, MBE (SCO)

P McGinley (IRL)

C Montgomerie, OBE (SCO)

H Stenson (SWE)

The All Time European Tour Winners Country

6

33

32

5

7

1

24

10

22

16

34

13

23

27

1 ARGENTINA
Number of wins: 30
Number of winners: 11
Leading performers:
Eduardo Romero (8); Angel Cabrera (5)
Vicente Fernandez (4)

2 AUSTRALIA
Number of wins: 102
Number of winners: 35
Leading performers: Greg Norman (14);
Graham Marsh (10); Rodger Davis (7)

3 AUSTRIA
Number of wins: 2
Number of winners: 1
Leading performer: Markus Brier (2)

4 BELGIUM
Number of wins: 1
Number of winners: 1
Leading performer:
Phillipe Toussaint (1)

5 BRAZIL
Number of wins: 1
Number of winners: 1
Leading performer: Jamie Gonzalez (1)

6 CANADA
Number of wins: 3
Number of winners: 2
Leading performers: Mike Weir (2);
Jerry Anderson (1)

7 CHILE
Number of wins: 1
Number of winners: 1
Leading performer: Felipe Aguilar (1)

8 CHINA
Number of wins: 2
Number of winners: 2
Leading performers: Zhang Lian-wei,
Liang Wen-chong (1)

9 DENMARK
Number of wins: 21
Number of winners: 7
Leading performers: Thomas Björn (9);
Anders Hansen, Søren Kjeldsen(3),
Søren Hansen, Steen Tinning (2)

10 ENGLAND
Number of wins: 249
Number of winners: 78
Leading performers: Nick Faldo (30);
Lee Westwood (20); Mark James (18);
Howard Clark (11)

11 FIJI
Number of wins: 13
Number of winners: 1
Leading performer: Vijay Singh (13)

12 FINLAND
Number of wins: 2
Number of winners: 1
Leading performer: Mikko Ilonen (2)

13 FRANCE
Number of wins: 22
Number of winners: 10
Leading performers: Thomas Levet (5);
Grégory Bourdy, Grégory Havret,
Jean-Francois Remesy (3);
Christian Cévaër, Raphaël Jacquelin,
Jean Van de Velde (2)

14 GERMANY
Number of wins: 56
Number of winners: 6
Leading performers: Bernhard Langer
(42); Alex Cejka,Martin Kaymer (4);
Sven Strüver (3)

15 INDIA
Number of wins: 7
Number of winners: 3
Leading performers: Arjun Atwal, Jeev
Milkha Singh (3); SSP Chowrasia (1)

16 IRELAND
Number of wins: 44
Number of winners: 14
Leading performers: Padraig
Harrington (14); Des Smyth (8);
Eamonn Darcy, Paul McGinley,
Christy O'Connor Jnr (4)

17 ITALY
Number of wins: 11
Number of winners: 6
Leading performers: Costantino
Rocca (5); Baldovino Dassu (2);
Emanuele Canonica, Massimo
Mannelli, Francesco Molinari,
Massimo Scarpa (1)

18 JAPAN
Number of wins: 1
Number of winners: 1
Leading performer: Isao Aoki (1)

MOST VICTORIES BY PLAYER
THE TOP TEN

1.	Seve Ballesteros	50
2.	Bernhard Langer	42
3.	Tiger Woods	38
4.	Colin Montgomerie	31
5.	Nick Faldo	30
6.	Ian Woosnam	29
7.	Ernie Els	24
8.	José Maria Olazábal	23
9.	Sam Torrance	21
10.	Lee Westwood	20